Students' Book

the *Pre-Intermediate*

CHOICE

Sue Mohamed and Richard Acklam

Longman

Unit	Structures	Vocabulary	English in Action
0 **What do you know?**	• Revision of positive and negative forms of: *be/can/have got/do/like*	Revision of lexical sets: food, clothes, colours, rooms, family, weather, places, body, transport, jobs	
1 **Person to person** (Focus on the Present)	• Question forms: inversion and auxiliary *do* • Likes and dislikes (1): *like/love/enjoy/ prefer/don't like/hate* + *-ing* form • Present Simple (routine) • *Could you . . .?* (requests)	• The alphabet • Work and free time activities (1) • Jobs (1) • Question words: *What/Where/ When/How/How many?* • Greetings and health	Making a class magazine
2 **Lookalikes** (Focus on the Past)	• Comparatives + *(not) as . . . as; the same as; different from* • Past Simple (irregular verbs) • *Be like* vs *look like* • *Used to*	• Clothes and accessories • Describing people (1 + 2) • Face and body	Conducting a survey about relationships
3 **Traveller's check** (Focus on the Future)	• *Going to* vs *will* • *Really/quite* + verb • Likes and dislikes (2): *can't stand* + *-ing* form • Superlatives • *Instead of* + noun	• Travel objects • Transport + *get on/off/into/out of* • Holiday activities	Writing for a travel brochure
4 **Necessary business** (Focus on Modals)	• Degrees of obligation (1): *should/have to/ don't have to* • Advice (1): *should/shouldn't* • Possessive pronouns: *mine/yours/hers, his/ours/theirs* • Suggestions (1): *Let's/Why don't we . . .?*	• Work and free time activities (2) • Jobs (2) • Personal qualities	Planning a new business
5 **Consolidation** • Across cultures: lifestyles	• Thinking about learning: strategies	• Language in context: eating out	
6 **Obsessions** (Focus on the Present)	• Present Simple vs Present Continuous (habits vs now) • Adverbs of frequency (word order): *always/often/sometimes/occasionally/ never* • Likes and dislikes (3): *don't mind* + *-ing*	• Everyday actions • Sports (football) • Hobbies	Talking about a hobby
7 **Spotlight** (Focus on the Past)	• Present Perfect (experience) vs Past Simple • Past participles (1 + 2) • Present Perfect (recent past) +/– *just* • Subject/object pronouns and possessive adjectives • Suggestions (2): *How/What about . . .?* + *-ing* form	• Adjectives ending in *-ed/-ing* • Types of films	Planning an evening at the cinema
Movie time	Making movies		
8 **Consequences** (Focus on the Future)	• *So* vs *because* • *If/when* + future time • *If* + present + *will* (first conditional) • *Definitely/probably* + *will* (word order)	• Education • Examinations	Finding out about English exams
9 **Face value** (Focus on Modals)	• Logical deduction: *must be/might be/ can't be* • *Look* vs *look like* • *Really/very/quite* + adjective • Present Perfect (indefinite time) +/– *yet/ already*	• Describing people (3) • Music and concerts	Talking about and buying records
10 **Consolidation** • Across cultures: money	• Language in context: shopping	• Thinking about learning: approaches	

Unit		Structures	Vocabulary	English in Action
	Images	A visual imagination activity		
11	**Changes** (Focus on the Present)	• Present Perfect (unfinished past) • *For* vs *since* • *Been* vs *gone* • *Give* + two objects	• Life changes • Expressions of time	Emigrating and writing character references
12	**Memory** (Focus on the Past)	• Past Continuous (interrupted action) • Sequencers: *first/then/next/after that/ finally* • *Some/any* + countable/uncountable nouns • Infinitive of purpose	• Everyday objects • Products and shops	Improving your memory
13	**Time for politics** (Focus on the Future)	• Subject/object questions • *Will/won't* (promises) • *As soon as* + present + *will* • Present Continuous (future arrangements)	• Political leaders, systems and issues	Forming a political party
14	**Generation gap** (Focus on Modals)	• Degrees of obligation (2): *should/must* and *shouldn't/mustn't/don't have to* • *Too/enough* + adjective • *Although/but/however*	• Ways of expressing movement and change	Reading and writing poems
15	**Consolidation** • Across cultures: children • Language in context: corporal punishment • Thinking about learning: improving your memory			
16	**How much is too much?** (Focus on the Present)	• *Want* + object + infinitive • *When/as soon as/after/before* • *Who* in relative clauses • *A* vs *the* • *A lot of/much/many/none* + countable/ uncountable nouns	• Animals • Describing people (4) • Products and packages	Going to the bank
17	**The man who died twice** (Focus on the Past)	• Present and Past Simple passive forms • *By/with* + passive forms • Past participles (3) • *I think so/I don't think so* • *So* vs *such*	• Causes of death • Punctuation marks	Finding out about local history
	Murder	A board game		
18	**What would you give up?** (Focus on the Future)	• Speculation: *would* (vs *could*) • Agreeing and disagreeing • *If* + past + *would* (second conditional) • *Make* (someone) *feel* + adjective	• Household equipment • Types of music	Planning a musical tour of Europe
19	**Do the right thing** (Focus on Modals)	• *Say* vs *tell* • Reported vs direct speech (statements) • Advice (2): *If I were you . . .*	• Large numbers • Customer rights	Making complaints
20	**Consolidation** • Across cultures: marriage • Language in context: love • Thinking about learning: outside the classroom – Radio Magazine			

An extended map of the contents of *The Pre-Intermediate Choice* can be found at the front of the Teacher's Book, featuring:
• the pronunciation syllabus
• the skills work, unit by unit
• the detailed contents of each Consolidation Unit

1 Put one of these words in each column below.

father   black   bank   taxi   kitchen
egg   windy   head   scarf   dentist

food	clothes	colours	rooms	family	weather	places	body	transport	jobs

2 Add two or three other words you know to each column.

3 Speak to two other students. Add their words to your columns.

4 Describe the photographs above to the other students.

   Example: There's a man in the kitchen. He . . .

5 Complete the verb tables with the correct form of each verb.

Be

I	. . .		Maria/Antonio.
You/We/They	. . .	(not)	married.
She/He/(It)	. . .		30.

Can

I/You			swim.
She/He/(It)	. . .	(not)	speak English.
We/They			stay out late.

Have got

I/You			a big family.
We/They	. . .	(not) got	a new car.
She/He/(It)	. . .		a headache.

Do (positive)

I/You		the shopping	
We/They	. . .	homework	regularly.
She/He/(It)	. . .	sport	

Do (negative)

I/You				the shopping.
We/They	. . .	not	do	homework.
She/He/(It)	. . .			sport.

Like (positive)

I/You/We/They	. . .	tea.
She/He/(It)	. . .	watching TV.

Like (negative)

I/You/We/They	. . .			tea.
She/He/(It)	. . .	not	like	watching TV.

6 Talk to another student. Which verb do you use with:

names?	likes/dislikes?	age?	family?
abilities?	possessions?	jobs?	
housework?	marital status?	illnesses?	

7 Write ten sentences about yourself. Use some of the verbs above.

Example: My name is . . .
I have got . . .

1 *Person to person*

The alphabet; personal questions; question words

1 Preparation

1 Check the names of students you don't know, like this:

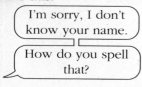

I'm sorry, I don't know your name.

How do you spell that?

Greta.

G.R.E.T.A.

2 Put your class in alphabetical order by first names.

Example: Anna, Antoine, Bjorn, . . .

2 Speaking

Read the information under the photographs in the article on page 7. Which of these questions did the interviewer ask each person?

a) What's your name?
b) Where do you come from?
c) Are you married?
d) Have you got any children?
e) What do you do?
f) What languages can you speak?
g) How old are you?
h) When did you start learning English?
i) How many English-speaking countries have you been to?

Pronunciation: sentence stress

1 🖳 Listen to the questions above. Which word has main stress in each question?

Example: What's your <u>name</u>?

2 Ask another student some of the questions above.

3 Grammar: question forms

Question	Positive
a) What is your name?	My name is Paola.
b) Where do you come from?	I come from Brazil.

1 Look at questions a) and b) above. What's the difference in how they are made?

2 Now look at questions c) – i) in Exercise 2 Speaking.

Which questions are formed like a)?
Which questions are formed like b)?

3 Write questions for these answers.

1 . . .? No, but I can speak German and Spanish.
2 . . .? Yes, very much. I generally see one or two films a week.
3 . . .? Yes. One brother and two sisters.
4 . . .? My brother's 15 and my sisters are 20 and 21.
5 . . .? I usually go out with friends or stay at home and watch TV.
6 . . .? Quite near here. I've got a small two-bedroomed flat.

4 Work with another student. Use these prompts to make interesting questions to ask other students or your teacher.

Are you . . .?   What . . .?
Have you got . . .?   Where . . .?
Can you . . .?   When . . .?
Do you . . .?   How . . .?
Did you . . .?   How many . . .?

NB The alphabet

/eɪ/ A _ _ _
/iː/   B _ _ _ _ _ _
/e/   F _ _ _ _ _
/aɪ/ I _
/əʊ/ O
/uː/ Q _ _
/ɑː/ R

Put the other letters of the alphabet in the correct group.

THE GAMBIA Kadi Secka, 22, student in Banjul.

PERSON TO PERSON

HAVE YOU EVER WONDERED WHAT LIFE WOULD HAVE BEEN LIKE IF YOU'D BEEN BORN IN ANOTHER COUNTRY? NOW'S YOUR CHANCE TO FIND OUT.

1

....................................?
My job as a reporter means that I meet all sorts of people . I work five days a week and the hours are very flexible. There are lots of opportunities for travel. Because I speak Mandarin Chinese as well as Cantonese I'm often sent to mainland China . I find it very interesting to go there, but I'm always glad to get back here.

....................................?
Yes, he also works on the Post, but in the advertising department. He's British and we met here. My parents like him and we travel a lot together.

....................................?
I suppose I just go out with friends, usually to the same restaurants and bars in Tsim Sha Tsui. There are crowds everywhere at weekends and it's virtually impossible to visit the beaches.

....................................?
I studied in America and enjoyed my time there and I love travelling. But I stay in Hong Kong despite day-to-day difficulties – mainly because I want to be with my father, who is seventy. I guess I'm still very Chinese in that sense, despite my Western outlook.

2

....................................?
At home in Banjul with my mother and seventeen year old sister. Like most Gambian women, I will live in the family home until I get married.

....................................?
We do not start until we are eight in The Gambia. I am studying English (I speak English at school and Wollof at home), maths, science, French, agricultural science and cookery. I finish this summer, but if I have the chance I will go to another school for four years to take English, maths and science A levels.

....................................?
I would like to work as a businesswoman, maybe selling shoes imported from Western countries. Many people in The Gambia want to buy shoes, so I think it would be a good business.

....................................?
Five days a week I go to school from 8.30 to 2.30 pm. When I come home I rest until about 5 pm and then study for a bit. I enjoy listening to music at home or playing with my sister. I have many friends, all girls, and visit them at home. I'm a Muslim, so my social life does not include drinking. I don't smoke either.

3

....................................?
At the moment in London. I came over here because I knew people who were making a film and they offered me a job. I don't know how long I am going to stay.

....................................?
Yes, it's great. The people are fantastic. There is a very friendly atmosphere. It's good to be working for an independent company. There is also lots of opportunity for travel which I like. This is all excellent experience for me.

....................................?
It's OK. Actually, I haven't seen much outside of London. There are good and bad points about living in London, like living in any big city I suppose. But I prefer living in Paris. It's such a beautiful place. I like just walking around, sitting in cafés, drinking coffee and talking to friends.

....................................?
The thing I would really like to do is to start a film company with friends in Paris. Unfortunately it needs money, so we will have to wait for a while, but one day I hope it will be possible.

From Company

FRANCE Marc Bloy, 22, film producer in London.

HONG KONG Lulu Yu, 24, journalist for the South China Morning Post.

4 Reading

1 Work in three groups. Each group, read about a different person in the article above.

1 Which photograph goes with your part of the article?
2 Which group of questions below, A, B or C, was your person asked?
3 What was the order of these questions?

> A What is school like in your country?
> What is your daily routine?
> What are you going to do when you leave school?
> Where do you live?
>
> B What are your ambitions?
> What do you think of England?
> Where do you work?
> Do you enjoy what you do?
>
> C Have you got a boyfriend?
> What do you do at work?
> Would you like to live in another country?
> What do you do in your free time?

2 Read your part of the article again and write short answers to your four questions.

3 Work in groups of three with one student from group A, one from group B and one from group C. Tell the two other students about your part of the article. Listen to them and write the answers to their questions.

4 What do you think? Which person would you most like to know? Why?

5 Grammar: -ing form

> Lulu Yu: *. . . and I love travelling.*
> Kadi Secka: *I enjoy listening to music or playing with my sister.*
> Marc Bloy: *I prefer living in Paris. I like just walking around, sitting in cafés, drinking coffee and talking to friends.*

1 Look at the sentences above and answer these questions.

1 Which verbs are followed by verb + *ing*? What do they have in common?

2 How do you say the opposite of the sentences above?

2 Tell another student how you feel about these things.

travelling by plane	writing letters	driving
going to museums	getting up early	cooking

6 Vocabulary: work and free time

1 Put these words into one or both of the columns below.

- teaching in a secondary school
- dancing
- listening to music
- going to the theatre
- writing detective novels
- directing films for TV
- drinking in bars
- driving taxis
- eating in restaurants with friends
- reporting stories for TV news
- reading novels
- playing football for Real Madrid
- going to the cinema

Jobs	Free time activities
teaching in a secondary school *dancing*	*dancing*

2 Name the person who does each job.

Example: teaching in a secondary school – a teacher

3 📼 **Listen. Check your answers and mark the stress. How do you pronounce er/or at the end of these words?**

Example: a 'teacher

4 Work with other students. List other jobs that end in *er/or*. What do these people do at work?

Example: A teacher teaches.

5 Ask other students about their work and free time, like this:

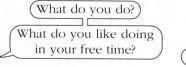

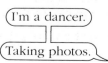

7 Writing

1 Listen and write the name, address and telephone number your teacher reads. If necessary, ask for clarification, like this:

> Could you say that again, please?

> Could you spell that, please?

2 Work in pairs and take it in turns to dictate names, addresses and telephone numbers to your partner.

STUDENT A: Dictate the business card on this page.

STUDENT B: Dictate the business card on page 124.

DOYLES LTD

Melissa Mainwaring
MANAGING DIRECTOR

48-50 Loughborough Avenue
Falmouth
CORNWALL
TR3 5JT
tel: 0326 250425

3 Now dictate your own name, address and telephone number to your partner.

> **NB** *a/an* + jobs
>
> I'm *a* doctor.
> I'm *an* actor.
>
> **What do you do?**

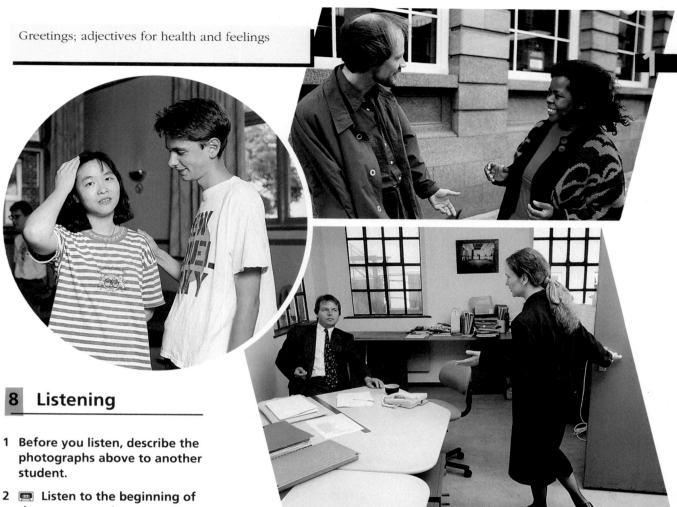

8 Listening

1 Before you listen, describe the photographs above to another student.

2 🖳 Listen to the beginning of three conversations.

  1 Match the photographs to the conversations.
  2 For each conversation decide if the people are:
  a) business colleagues
  b) people who don't know each other very well
  c) good friends

3 Listen again and answer these questions.

In which conversation does someone:
  a) know the other person's brother?
  b) talk about a holiday?
  c) return to work?

4 Listen again and answer these questions.

  1 How do the people greet each other in each conversation? What word/phrase do they use?
  2 How do the people say how they are feeling? Write another word or phrase they use which means:

++	+	–	– –
very well	not bad	not very well	terrible
. . .	. . .	. . .	. . .

5 🖳 Listen and repeat the phrases above with feeling.

6 Add other words/phrases with similar meanings to the list.

Speaking

1 Listen to conversation 1 again. Then practise it with a partner. Change the names, the day of the week and the place.

2 Continue the conversation and ask more questions about your partner's holiday.

9

ENGLISH IN ACTION

You are going to interview another student and write an article for a class magazine. First, find out which direct questions are polite.

1 Look at the questions below. In your country, who can/can't you ask these questions? Think about these people:

a colleague at work   a child
a good friend   a person in your family
a person you meet for the first time

- What's your name?
- How do you do?
- How old are you?
- How much do you earn?
- Are you married?
- Why haven't you got any children?
- How much did your watch cost?
- What do you think of the government?

2 Speak to other people about the English-speaking countries they know. What do they think? When are these questions polite?

Choose a student to interview.

3 Decide what questions you want to ask. Which topics interest you (eg. family, work, free time, etc.)? Ask your partner questions and take notes.

4 Write a short article about your partner, using your notes. Write a different paragraph for each topic.

5 Organise the articles and make your class magazine.

Read about the other students in your class.

Language review 1

1 -ing form (activities)

acting in plays
directing a company
reporting for a newspaper
designing clothes

driving buses
playing tennis
teaching languages

a Look at the activities on the left and name the job from each activity. Then mark the stress and say what each person does at work.

Example: She/he's an 'actor. She/he acts in plays.

2 Verbs

• + -ing form
Use verb + -ing form after like/love/prefer/enjoy/hate.

I/You/We/They	love	swimming.
She/He/(It)	loves	

• Questions with do
Use auxiliary do with regular verbs.

I/You/We/They	like	tea.	Do	I/you/we/they	like tea?
She/He/(It)	likes		Does	she/he/(it)	

• Inverted questions
Invert the verb and the subject with be/can/have got.

Be

I	am	late.	Am	I	late?
You/We/They	are		Are	you/we/they	
She/He/It	is		Is	she/he/it	

Can

I/You We/They She/He/(It)	can dance.	Can	I/you/ we/they/ she/he/(it)	dance?

Have got

I/You/ We/They	have	got a car.	Have	I/you/ we/they	got a car?
She/He/(It)	has		Has	she/he/(it)	

b Look at the chart below. For each person, answer these questions in complete sentences.

1 What does she/he prefer, swimming or skiing?
2 What does she/he like doing most?
3 What does she/he hate doing?
4 Which two people enjoy dancing?
5 Which two people don't like skiing?

Name	Loves	Likes	Hates
Odette	dancing	swimming	skiing
Ali	skiing	swimming	dancing
Shelly	swimming	dancing	skiing

c Find one mistake in each question below, then write the correct question.

Example: Do you like go to the cinema? ✗
Do you like going to the cinema? ✓

1 Do you have got any children?
2 Are you student?
3 How much languages do you speak?
4 What do you doing at the weekends?
5 Can you to speak English very well?
6 When did you started learning English?
7 How old have you?

d Match each of these answers to a question in exercise c above.

Example: Do you like going to the cinema? – h

a No, I'm a doctor.
b Nearly thirty-five.
c No, just a little.
d Go shopping and visit friends.
e A year ago.
f Yes, three.
g Two. Spanish and English.
h Yes, at the weekend.

3 Could you ...? (requests)

Ask people politely, like this:

Could you	+ verb	+ please?
Could you	help,	please?

e Write requests. What do you say when you want:

1 the window open?   4 someone to spell their name?
2 someone to repeat?   5 attention in a shop?
3 someone's address?   6 a return phone call?

Seeing DOUBLE

Seconds away . . . as over 1500 perfect pairs meet in Twinsburg, Ohio, for their annual identical twins competition, we preview the world's biggest meeting of identical twins.

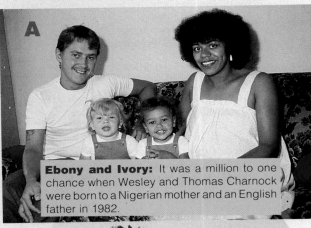

Ebony and Ivory: It was a million to one chance when Wesley and Thomas Charnock were born to a Nigerian mother and an English father in 1982.

Second Sight: Faye Gallo and Sue Gallo Baugher, 64, of Warren Ohio, have the same taste in clothes. On shopping trips, one tries the clothes on, the other decides.

Goss Bros: Matt and Luke (or is it Luke and Matt?) have become the nation's most pair-fect pop duo: singing their way to teenage hearts.

Double Trouble: Living 30 miles apart, Barbara and Daphne first met when they were 33 at Kings Cross Station in identical outfits.

The Skull Sisters: a painting duo from Miami. Their 3-D pictures of Cuban life are only a little less colourful than their outrageously identical dress sense.

The Thompson Twins: Gareth and Nicholas, from Nottinghamshire, who at the age of six, surprised doctors by needing exactly the same kidney operation.

From *She*

1 Preparation

1 Work with another student. Look at the magazine page opposite and answer these questions.

1 Which pairs are wearing matching hats?
2 What other matching clothes/accessories are they wearing?
3 What clothes/accessories are people in your class wearing? Who is wearing matching clothes?

2 Read about the twins and answer these questions. Which pair:

1 always go clothes shopping together?
2 are artists?
3 are pop singers?
4 didn't live together as children?
5 surprised doctors at their birth?
6 had the same medical problem?

2 Grammar: comparatives

> Gareth is bigg*er than* Nicholas.
> Gareth is heav*ier than* Nicholas.
> Gareth is *more* independent *than* Nicholas.

1 Read the sentences above about the differences between the Thompson twins. Answer these questions.

1 Is Gareth on the left or right of the photograph?
2 How do you make the comparatives of:

a) one-syllable adjectives?
b) two-syllable adjectives ending in *y*?
c) adjectives of two, three or more syllables?

2 Now compare Nicholas to Gareth. Write sentences with the same meaning as the ones above. Begin each sentence like this:

Nicholas is . . .

3 Write sentences comparing two people you know. Use comparatives of some of these adjectives:

tall/short   shy/confident
old/young   friendly/unfriendly
tidy/untidy   ambitious/unambitious
hardworking/lazy

4 Look at the pairs of sentences below. Is the meaning of the two sentences in each box the same or different?

> 1 Gareth is *different from* Nicholas.
> Gareth is not *the same as* Nicholas.

> 2 Gareth is *the same* age *as* Nicholas.
> Gareth is *as* old *as* Nicholas.

> 3 Gareth is bigg*er than* Nicholas.
> Gareth is*n't as* big *as* Nicholas.

> 4 Gareth is *more* independent *than* Nicholas.
> Nicholas is *less* independent *than* Gareth.

5 Complete these sentences about the other twins, using comparatives.

1 Matt is taller than Luke.
  Luke isn't . . . Matt.
  He is . . . Matt.
2 The Skull sisters are less famous than Bros.
  Bros are . . . the Skull sisters.
3 Wesley is a different colour from Thomas.
  He isn't . . . Thomas.
4 Barbara and Daphne have both got short hair.
  Daphne's hair is as . . . Barbara's.
5 Barbara's hair is dark brown and Daphne's hair is light brown.
  Daphne's hair isn't as . . . Barbara's.

Pronunciation: /ə/ in unstressed words

1 ▣ Listen to the completed sentences. Mark the stressed word in these expressions and the unstressed sound /ə/.

      /ə/ /ə/
'taller than
as tall as   different from
shorter than   the same as
less famous than   as short as
more famous than   (isn't) as dark as

2 Work with another student. Decide which pair of twins are the most identical. Say why you didn't choose the others.

3 Talk to other students about a country or town you know well. Compare the eating habits, transport, weather and people in the different places.

3 Reading

1 Before you read, match these words from the newspaper article in column A to their meanings in column B.

A	B
1 to adopt	a) to give a part to another person
2 to arrange	b) a sofa and two armchairs
3 the local council	c) a cupboard for clothes
4 a three-piece suite	d) to stop seeing/contacting people
5 to have a miscarriage	e) the government of the area you live in
6 a wardrobe	f) to make plans
7 to share	g) to lose a baby before it is born
8 to lose touch	h) to take another person's child into your family

2 Read Barbara and Daphne's story in the article below. What is surprising about it?

3 Work with another student. List all the similarities and coincidences you can find in the sisters' lives.

Grammar: Past Simple

1 Complete the table with irregular verbs from the text.

Present	Past Simple
know	knew
be	was
meet	. . .
come	. . .
forget	. . .
can	. . .
put	. . .
find	. . .
have	. . .
go	. . .
say	. . .
buy	. . .

2 Retell the story using the verbs above.

Daily Mail, Monday, January 30

IDENTICAL TWINS REUNITED AFTER A LIFETIME APART

Identical Strangers on Platform 8

Identical twins Barbara and Daphne didn't know each other until they met nine years ago. When they were born they were separated and adopted by different families. But when they met, it was just like looking into a mirror. After a separation of more than 40 years, they look alike, talk alike and even laugh alike.

"We arranged to meet at King's Cross. When the train came in I was standing exactly where Daphne was waiting to get off," says Barbara. "As the train stopped we were right opposite each other. We walked straight off together, talking and laughing like old friends and forgot all about our husbands. We both work for local councils and met our husbands at dances. They both have similar jobs - my Frank is a shop manager and Daphne's Peter is a marketing manager. Both are quiet,

hardworking men."

The two husbands in question couldn't believe their eyes. They had married one woman and suddenly here was another one - exactly the same. "It was incredible," says Barbara's husband, Frank. "Even the gestures - the way they both put their hands to their mouths when they laughed - were identical."

Barbara and Daphne found that their halls were painted the same and they had the same three-piece suites in their living rooms. They had both had one miscarriage, followed by two sons and then a daughter. They both drink their coffee black, no sugar and half cold. When Daphne went down to Barbara's house in Dover for a big reunion party she packed her black dress with flowers, beige dress and brown velvet jacket. Barbara, not

knowing this, opened her wardrobe, and said to Daphne, "Well, I could either wear my black dress with flowers, or my beige, with my brown velvet jacket."

"I don't really know what it's like to be a sister - sharing clothes and boyfriends, etc. So Barbara's more like a best friend. When we phone each other in the evenings we're nearly always cooking exactly the same meals for supper. Three times we bought the same books on the same day. But unlike friends, who you can lose touch with, we definitely won't lose touch - now we've found each other."

From The Daily Mail

4 Speaking

Barbara *looks like* Daphne.
They *look like* each other.

1 Look at the sentences above and at the first paragraph in the newspaper article. Find other things that Barbara and Daphne do the same.

2 Talk to other students about people you are like.

1 Who do you look like in your family? Whose nose/eyes, etc. have you got?

2 What things do you do exactly like other members of your family and/or your friends?

5 Listening

1 Before you listen, match the words below to the parts of the body and face they can go with.

hair eyes nose ears skin figure legs

straight/curly   small/medium/large
fair/dark   black/grey/blond
long/short   blue/brown/green
slim/thin/fat

2 Look at the photographs of the actress Cher. Answer these questions with other students.

1 What do you think? Which photograph was taken before/after she had cosmetic surgery?

2 In which photograph does she look younger/ more sophisticated/more attractive?

3 Which photograph do you prefer? Why?

4 Do you think cosmetic surgery is a good idea? Why/Why not?

3 🖳 Listen to two women discussing Cher's cosmetic surgery and answer the questions.

1 Are they generally for or against cosmetic surgery?

2 Do they think Cher looks better or worse now?

4 Listen again and answer these questions.

1 Which parts of Cher's body do they talk about?

2 Which words do they use to describe them now? What were they like before?

6 Grammar: *used to*

She *used to* be a hippy.

1 Look at the sentence above from the women's conversation.

1 Does it mean a) or b) below?
   a) She was a hippy in the past and she still is.
   b) She was a hippy in the past but she isn't now.

2 How do you make the negative of *used to*?

3 How do you make the question form?

2 Complete these sentences about Cher with *used to/didn't use to*.

1 She . . . wear flowers in her hair.
2 She . . . be very confident.
3 She . . . think she was beautiful.
4 Her nose . . . be as straight as it is now.
5 Her hair . . . be straighter than it is now.
6 Her legs . . . be fatter.

3 Tell another student how *you* have changed. Think about one or two of the areas below.

Example: (work) I *used to* enjoy my job but now I don't because . . .

politics   religion   looks/character
money   work   friendships/relationships

4 Tell the class something surprising about your partner's past.

NB *be like* vs *look like*

a) What does she *look like*? She's tall.
b) What *is* she *like*? She's attractive and very friendly.

1 Which question refers to personality and appearance, a) or b)?

2 Which question refers to appearance only?

15

*chat*living

Mirror Image

Do you look like your best friend or partner? Do you know couples who look alike? How far are we attracted to people with the same appearance?

It's amazing how, when you look at your friends and family, so many couples look the same. And it's not only couples - best friends often have similar hair, similar taste in clothes and even similar noses! The psychologist Doctor David Lewis believes "We make good relationships with people who look like us."

To discover how well you and your best friend/partner match up, complete this questionnaire.

Lookalike Questionnaire

1 Eyes

You
a) blue b) brown c) green d) other...

Your best friend/partner
a) blue b) brown c) green d) other...

2 Hair

You
a)... b)... c)... d)...

Your best friend/partner
a)... b)... c)... d)...

Find out about people and their

From Chat

relationships.

1 Read the beginning of the article. What does Doctor Lewis, the psychologist, suggest about our choice of friends/partners?

2 Find out if this is true! Work with other students. Make a questionnaire to ask people about their friends/partners. Add at least four more categories to the questionnaire above.

3 Ask at least five people your questions. Ask them about their own appearance and also about their best friend/partner's appearance.

4 Report your results to the class. How many answers suggest Dr Lewis is right? How many suggest he isn't?

Language review 2

1 Comparatives

- **One-syllable adjectives**

B is older *than* A but *not as* old *as* C.

- **Two-syllable adjectives, ending in *y***

A is happi*er than* B and *as* happy *as* C.

- **Two, three or more syllable adjectives**

C is *more* intelligent *than* A and B.
A and B are *less* intelligent *than* C.

- ***The same as/different from***

A's hair is *the same* colour *as* B's but a *different* colour *from* C's.

a **Look at the pictures and complete the sentences.**

Example: D is *taller than* E but not *as tall as* F.

1 D is (heavy) . . . F but not . . . E.
2 E is (rich) . . . D but . . .
3 F's job is . . .
4 E works . . .

b **Complete the sentences with *than, as* or *from*.**

Example: Gold is more expensive *than* silver.

1 I'm not as tired . . . I was yesterday.
2 She earns more . . . me.
3 He gave me the same present . . . you.
4 He isn't as unattractive . . . he thinks.
5 The film is very different . . . the book.
6 This exercise is easier . . . you think!

2 Verbs

- ***Used to* (only for past time)**

Used to **says something happened regularly in the past but no longer happens now.**

Positive

I/You/We/They	*used to* smoke.
She/He/It	

Negative

I/You/We/They	*did not*	*use to* smoke.
She/He/It	*(didn't)*	

Question and short answers

Did	I/you/we/they	*use to* smoke?	Yes, they *did.*
	she/he/it		No, they *didn't.*

- **Verb + *like***

Look like (for appearance)

I/You/We/They	*look*	*like* a film star.
She/He/It	*looks*	

Be like (for appearance + personality)

I	*am*	*like* my brother, kind and attractive.
You/We/They	*are*	
She/He/It	*is*	

c **When Sebastian was a student he was relaxed, happy and healthy. Now he is a businessman and life has changed. Complete these sentences comparing his past and present life.**

Example: He . . . to smoke but . . .
He *didn't use* to smoke but *he smokes now.*

1 He . . . do a lot of exercise but . . .
2 He . . . drink very much but . . .
3 He . . . have a lot of free time but . . .
4 He . . . enjoy life but . . .

d **Write questions to ask Sebastian more about his student life. Find out:**

1 where he used to live.
2 what type of music he used to listen to.
3 what he used to do at the weekend.
4 if he used to have enough money.
5 if he often used to go to the cinema.

e **Write complete answers to the questions yourself. Think about your life when you were much younger.**

f **Complete these sentences with the correct form of *be* or *look*.**

1 I don't . . . like any of my brothers or sisters.
2 What . . . the weather like? Hot and sunny.
3 She . . . like her mother – charming and intelligent.
4 The actress makes a lot of money because she . . . like Marilyn Monroe.
5 What. . . your teacher like? She's nice.

3 Traveller's check

1 Preparation

1 Look at the photograph above. Which of these things can you see? Which can't you see?

a walkman	traveller's cheques
a passport	foreign currency
a briefcase	suntan lotion
a map	a camera
an alarm clock	sunglasses
a toothbrush	an electric shaver

2 Put the vocabulary in the correct column below. Which words don't go in either column?

Two separate words	Compound words
alarm clock	*walkman*

3 📖 Listen. Where is the stress on the compound words?

2 Listening

1 📖 Listen to a conversation between Martine and her friend, Carl.

1 Who is going away?
2 Where is she/he going? How is she/he going to travel?
3 What is she/he going to do when she/he gets there?
4 What is the other person going to do?

2 Listen again. Which things in the photograph above does Martine decide to take?

Pronunciation: letter 'a'; saying lists

/eɪ/	/ɑː/	/ɔː/ /ə/	/æ/
I'll take my sunglasses, my walkman and a map.

1 📖 Listen to the five different ways of pronouncing the letter 'a' above. Find other words with 'a' in them in Exercise 1 Preparation. Group them by sound.

2 Look at the sentence above again.

1 How many times does *and* appear in the list?
2 What do you put instead of *and* in the middle of lists?
3 In your language, does your voice go up or down:
   a) at the end of lists?
   b) as you list each thing?

3 Listen again and repeat Martine's sentence. Does she say the list in the same way as you?

4 Work with other students. Take it in turns to list what you'll take on holiday. Remember what other students say and add one new thing.

Example: STUDENT A: I'll take a camera.

STUDENT B: I'll take a camera and a walkman.

STUDENT C: I'll take a camera, a walkman and a . . .

LEICESTER TO LONDON EVERY 30* MINUTES.

*Weekday Service.

INTERCITY

3 Grammar: *going to* vs *will*

1 **Look at the advertisement for British Rail. How often do trains go from Leicester to London?**

2 **Read the advertisement and answer these questions about the woman.**

1 Which town is she going to travel to?
2 What makes her decide to catch a later train?
3 What does she think when she changes her mind?

3 **Read these sentences and answer the questions below.**

> A: I am going to catch the 10 o'clock train.
> B: I'll catch the 10 o'clock train.

1 Did A make the decision:
   a) before speaking?
   b) at the time of speaking?
2 Did B make the decision:
   a) before speaking?
   b) at the time of speaking?

4 **Complete these dialogues with *is/are going* to or *will*. Use contracted forms.**

1 FRANK: Jane, can you possibly take me to the station this evening?
  JANE: Of course I (1) . . . take you. I'd be pleased to.
  Later
  PETE: Frank, would you like me to take you to the station?
  FRANK: No thanks, Pete. Jane (2) . . . take me.

2 SOPHIE: Emma, Dave, have you decided what to do this evening?
  DAVE: Yes, we (3) . . . meet Jane and go to the disco in town.
  SOPHIE: What a good idea. I (4) . . . come too.
  EMMA: Great! We (5) . . . have a meal first. Come with us!

5 **Practise the dialogues with other students.**

> **NB** *going to go*
>
> a) I'm going *to catch* the 10 o'clock train.
> b) I'm going (*to go*) to London.
>
> *To catch* is necessary in sentence a).
> *To go* isn't necessary in sentence b).
>
> **Why? In which sentence is the verb *go* repeated, a) or b)?**

4 Vocabulary: transport

1 Answer these questions with other students.

1 What does a passenger catch at these places?

  a bus stop   a station   a coach station
  a taxi rank an airport an underground station

2 Which forms of transport mentioned do you:
  a) *get into* at the beginning of a journey?
  b) *get out of* at the end?
  c) *get on* at the beginning of a journey?
  d) *get off* at the end?

2 Work with another student. Find eight differences between picture A and picture B.

STUDENT A: Describe picture A on page 124.
STUDENT B: Describe picture B on page 126.

3 Ask other students what they are going to do after class. Where are they going? How are they going to get there?

5 Speaking

1 Talk to another student and answer these questions about holidays.

1 Where are you going to spend your next holiday? If you haven't decided, where would you like to go?
2 Which of the activities below do you like doing most/least on holiday? What other things do you like doing?

eating out	visiting museums
swimming	visiting historical sites
shopping	going on organised tours
going for walks	taking photographs
going to discos	buying souvenirs
sunbathing	

2 Talk to other students. How many of you feel the same way about each activity? List things you agree on in the correct column.

++ We really enjoy	+ We quite like	– – We can't stand

6 Reading

Read the article opposite about exotic holidays and complete this chart.

	Interesting things to see/do	Things to buy	Best time to go
Sri Lanka			
Cairo			
Bangkok			

Grammar: superlatives

The best time to go is in December.

1 Read the example sentence above and answer these questions.

1 What is the adjective of the irregular superlative *best*?
2 Find the opposite of *best* in the text about Bangkok. What is it describing?

2 Work with another student.

1 Find the superlatives in the texts which say what is most special about each place.
2 List the adjectives they come from. How are the superlatives formed for each adjective? Discuss any 'rules' you can see.
3 Make sentences about the places below, using superlatives. Use a word from each box once only.

Example: Bangkok is the hottest place in Thailand.

Bangkok	high	place	Asia
The Nile	large	river	France
Paris	long	country	the world
China	hot	mountain	Africa
Everest	populated	city	Thailand

Exotic Spots

Sri Lanka

Sri Lanka is one of the friendliest and most beautiful islands in the world. There is something here for everyone: the ruins of ancient cities, the green tea plantations where nearly half of the world's best tea is produced, and 1000 miles of golden beaches. Prices throughout the country are incredibly cheap and precious stones, delicate blue sapphires, are a great buy. Go any time. The weather is always good.

- **Prices for 14 nights with Cosmos (061 480 5799) start from £419**

Cairo

Cairo is fantastic! You'll never forget a holiday in the largest city in Africa. See the gold mask of Tutankhamen, the beauty of the Sphinx and the oldest pyramids in the Middle East. This is a world of bazaars, churches and mosques where the people are some of the happiest and friendliest you'll ever meet. Cairo is great value for money; from local crafts, carpets and gold jewellery to transport and good restaurants. It's best not to go from June to August when it's terribly hot and remember to get your visa in good time.

- **One week with Thomson (071 387 8484) costs from £417**

Bangkok

Officially the hottest city in the world, Bangkok, the capital of Thailand, is a good introduction to the Far East. The most sophisticated shops, hotels and nightclubs contrast with crowded streets and colourful markets. Specialities to buy include silk, jewellery and fake 'Rolex' watches for about £10! As well as the fabulous floating market in the photograph, you can visit the Grand Palace of the Thai royal family and over 300 religious temples. To avoid the worst heat and humidity, visit Bangkok in the cool season from November to February.

- **Intasun (0274 760011) offers 14 nights' holiday from £509**

From *Best*

7 Speaking

1 Choose a place from the article to visit next holiday. Write the answers to these questions.

1 Which place seems the most exciting to you?
2 How would you like to travel there?
3 Which month would you like to go?

2 Ask other students where/how/when they are going on holiday. Find the student who wants the most similar holiday to you.

3 Work with the student you found. Make changes to your plans so you can go on holiday together.

Example: I'll go in June *instead of* December.

4 Decide what information you need before booking your holiday. List questions to ask the travel company. Think about these things:

price   weather   time of departure/arrival
clothes   transport   hotel facilities

5 Work with a different student. Take it in turns to phone the travel agent. Begin and end your conversation like this:

TRAVEL AGENT: Hello, Cosmos. Can I help you?
CUSTOMER: Oh, hello. I am phoning to ask . . .
. . .
CUSTOMER: OK, that seems to be everything. Thank you for your help.
TRAVEL AGENT: Not at all. Goodbye.

Prepare to write an article about your country/town for a travel brochure.

1 Make questions from the prompts below.

Example: What/large/city/your country?
What is the largest city in your country?

1 What/interesting/tourist sights?
2 Who/famous/singer or entertainer?
3 What/typical/food?
4 What/popular/drink?
5 What/good/things/to buy?
6 When/good/time/to visit?

2 Discuss the answers to your questions with other students from your town/country.

3 Write complete answers to your questions.

Example: Lisbon is the largest city in Portugal.

4 Read the instructions below and write your article.

1 Choose the most interesting sentences for your article.
2 Decide what order you want to put the sentences in.
3 Link sentences if you can with *and/or/but/because*.

5 Show your work to other students. Which places would you most like to visit?

> **NB** *and/or/but/because*
>
> The Japanese eat a lot of rice *and* fish.
> They don't often eat meat *or* potatoes.
> Most of them like fish *but* they don't like meat.
> They eat a lot of fish *because* Japan is an island.
>
> **Which word, *and/or/but* or *because* links:**
> a) a positive and a negative idea?
> b) two positive ideas?
> c) two negative ideas?
> d) an idea and its reason?

Language review 3

1 Verbs: *going to* vs *will* (future)

Going to + verb (for decisions made before speaking)

Will + verb (for decisions made at the time of speaking)

A: We need some milk.

B: OK, *I'll go* to the shops and get some later.

Later

B: I'm *going to get* some milk. Do we need anything else?

A: Well, we haven't got any biscuits.

B: OK, *I'll buy* some at the shops.

a Rewrite these sentences using *going to* or *will*. Use contracted forms.

1 We *are going to/will* get married in June. We decided a month ago.
2 A: Why can't I see you at the weekend?
   B: I *am going to/will* visit some friends in Scotland.
3 A: We haven't got any sugar.
   B: OK. I *am going to/will* get some from the shops.
4 A: Why are you here?
   B: Because I *am going to/will* tell Mark tonight. I can't wait any longer.
5 A: I'm afraid Ms. Stephens isn't in at the moment.
   B: OK, I *am going to/will* leave her a message.

2 Superlatives

Comparatives compare two things or people. Superlatives compare more than two things or people.

• **Regular**

Adjective	Comparative	Superlative
cheap	cheaper (than)	the cheapest
hot	hotter (than)	the hottest
friendly	friendlier (than)	the friendliest
beautiful	more/less beautiful (than)	the most/least beautiful

• **Irregular**

Adjective	Comparative	Superlative
good	better (than)	the best
bad	worse (than)	the worst

b Complete these sentences with superlatives.

Example: Mike is . . . boy in the class. He is 2m tall.
Mike is *the tallest* boy in the class. He is 2m tall.

1 These shoes cost £100. They were . . . in the shop.
2 August is generally . . . month of the year in Britain. The temperature goes up to about 22°C.
3 The Romans made . . . roads in Europe. They go directly from A to B.
4 This is . . . car we've got at this price. It goes from 0 – 60 mph in 8 seconds.
5 They are . . . people I've ever met. They love to talk to foreigners and show you round the city.
6 Why don't you sit over there. That's . . . chair.
7 We decided to go by bus, not by train or plane, because it was . . . way to get there.
8 It's . . . film I've ever seen. It lasted three and a half hours.

3 *Quite/really* + verb

Use *quite/really* with verbs to make the meaning of the verb weaker or stronger.

+	I *quite* like apples.
++	I like oranges.
+++	I *really* like strawberries.

c Rephrase these sentences using *quite/really* and the verb in brackets.

Example: Playing football with my friends is great.
(like) I really like playing football with my friends.

1 I can't stand being late.
   (hate) . . .
2 I find watching TV is OK some of the time.
   (enjoy) . . .
3 Going shopping is all right when it's not too crowded.
   (like) . . .
4 Visiting good restaurants is my favourite holiday activity.
   (love) . . .
5 I find Pedro's mother very unpleasant.
   (can't stand) . . .

4 Necessary business

Degrees of obligation: *should/have to/don't have to*

1 Preparation

What do you think? Discuss the questions below with other students. What happens in your country?

When you visit friends for dinner is it	necessary	a good idea	not necessary
to dress up?			
to arrive on time?			
to take a small present?			
to help wash up?			
to ask before using the telephone?			
to leave after coffee?			

2 Grammar: *should/have to/don't have to*

1 Match the underlined words to their meanings.

1 a good idea   2 necessary   3 not necessary

a) I can't come to dinner because I <u>have to</u> work this evening.
b) I can come to dinner because I <u>don't have to</u> work this evening.
c) I <u>should</u> work but I'll come to dinner instead.

2 Write sentences about the situations in the chart above, using *should/have to/don't have to*.

Example: When you visit a friend for dinner in my country, you should dress up.

3 Pronunciation

/dʒʊ/
Do you have to work?
/duː/
Yes, I do.

1 📺 **Listen. Is *do* stressed in the question or answer above?**

2 📺 **Listen and write the positive and negative sentences you hear.**
1 Which word has main stress?
2 Which words can/can't you contract?

3 Ask about things you *have to/ don't have to* do everyday.

A: Do you have to get up early?
B: Yes, I do. I have to be up by 8 o'clock.

> **NB** *should* vs *have to*
>
> You *have to* phone first.
> You *should* phone first.
>
> **What comes immediately after *should*, another verb or *to*?**

From *The Daily Mail*

Tips for Tourists

In Britain tipping is common in many places, either because people are paid low wages or in appreciation of good service. In restaurants it is usual to leave 10% except where service is included, in which case it is at your discretion. Similarly at the hairdresser's and in taxis 10% is considered a fair amount although this will vary depending on the quality of service. Of course there are no fixed 'rules', some people never tip and others tip more. In general, however, tips are not given at the cinema, the theatre or in petrol stations. In hotels and at airports and stations, porters will expect a small tip for each piece of luggage carried. At Christmas it is not unusual for your milkman, dustman and postman to come round for their 'Christmas box'. This is your chance to give them money as a 'thank you' for their work throughout the year – how much is up to you.

4 Speaking

1 Read the text above about tipping in Britain and complete this chart.

Job	How much?

2 Talk to other students about tipping in your country. Answer these questions.

1 Is anything about tipping in Britain very different from your country?
2 In which of the situations below should you tip? How much should you tip:
  a) in a restaurant where the bill says 'service included'?
  b) at the hairdresser's?
  c) when they deliver food e.g. pizza to your house?
  d) when a porter carries your luggage at the station?
  e) at the end of a taxi ride?

3 Who else do you tip in your country?

4 What do you think? What are the advantages/disadvantages of tipping?

5 Vocabulary: jobs and qualities

1 Work with another student. Which of these jobs and qualities do you know between you?

1 Use the mini-dictionary on page 138 to check the meaning and pronunciation of words you are unsure of.
2 Mark the main stress on each word.

Example: a 'hairdresser

Jobs

a hairdresser	a waiter
a school teacher	a manager
a receptionist	a nurse
a social worker	a tennis player
an accountant	

Qualities

patient	punctual
organised	fair
creative	friendly
clever	understanding
fit	ambitious

2 Choose the quality you think is the most necessary for each job.

Example: A tennis player has to be fit.

3 Ask other students what they do or would like to do. What qualities are most necessary for their jobs?

4 Work with other students. List the qualities of a good teacher and put them in order of importance.

6 Reading

1 What do you think?

1 What things generally make time pass quickly/slowly for you?

2 Do you manage your time well or do you waste time?

2 Work with another student. Read these ideas for good management at work. For each suggestion, do you think a) or b)?

a) You should . . .

b) You don't have to . . .

- answer the phone when it rings.
- answer unimportant letters immediately.
- see people in *their* offices.
- plan your complete day in advance.
- always work with your door open.
- do a job yourself if you are responsible for the result.

3 Now read 'Managing your Time', written by some management consultants.

1 What do they say about the ideas above?

2 Is there anything you really disagree with?

Managing Your Time

1 Problem

The phone never stops ringing.

Solution

Plan 'open phone' and 'shut phone' time. You don't always have to answer it NOW. It is OK to be unavailable. How do you do your work otherwise?

2 Problem

Unimportant letters make your desk untidy. You answer them very late.

Solution

Try to answer them when you read them. Then you won't have to read them again. Plan time for opening and answering your post.

3 Problem

Visits from colleagues take too much time.

Solution

See them in their office. Then you can leave when *you* want.

4 Problem

Unrealistic planned time. You can't do what you plan in a day.

Solution

Everything takes longer than you think and other things happen. Leave at least 20% of the day unplanned.

5 Problem

Open door policy. You want people to know they can come and see you, but it's difficult to do your work with constant interruptions.

Solution

This can be dangerous! Plan 'open' and 'closed' times.

6 Problem

Too much work. You are responsible for too many things.

Solution

Delegate work to other people. Being responsible doesn't mean *you* have to do it.

7 Speaking

1 Discuss these questions with other students.

1 Which of these things do you enjoy doing? Which of them do you have to do?

- reading
- working
- shopping
- visiting parents
- seeing friends
- watching TV
- doing homework
- going to museums
- going to parties
- writing letters
- ironing

2 What other things do you have to do regularly? Do you enjoy doing them?

2 Look at the diary below and plan your time tomorrow.

3 Tell your partner one or two important things you plan to do. How long are you going to spend on each of them?

NDAY	9.00
	10.00
	11.00
	12.00
	13.00
	14.00
	15.00
	16.00
	17.00
	18.00
	19.00
	20.00
	21.00
	22.00
	23.00
	24.00

8 Listening

1 Before you listen, answer these questions.

1 When were you last late for work/class?
2 Why were you late? Did it matter?

2 ▦ Listen to the first interview between Jim, an office worker, and his manager. Answer these questions.

1 Is it the first time he is late? Does it matter?
2 What does the manager decide? Do you think it is fair?

3 ▦ Now listen to an alternative interview and answer these questions.

1 Why is Jim late? Does it matter?
2 What does the manager decide?

4 Discuss with other students.

1 In which interview does the manager do her job best? Why?
2 What advice would you give to the 'bad' manager?

Example: You should/shouldn't . . .

Grammar: possessive pronouns

> The others are doing your work as well as *theirs*.
> The manager is answering your letters as well as *hers*.
> My assistant is answering your phone as well as *his*.
> I'm looking after your clients as well as *mine*.

1 Look at the examples above and answer these questions.

1 Which two words could replace *theirs/hers/his/mine* in each sentence?
2 Why do we use the possessive pronoun?

2 Complete the chart with possessive pronouns.

my	mine	our	. . .
your	. . .	your	. . .
her	. . .	their	. . .
his	. . .		

3 Use possessive pronouns to play this game.

1 Everyone give the teacher a different personal possession.
2 Tell another student who each thing belongs to. Point at the person. Don't say her/his name. How many did you get right?

4 Take your possession back when your teacher asks whose it is.

Example: TEACHER: Whose is this pen?
YOU: It's mine.

| You are going to plan a new business. | Some of you are business people who want to borrow money to start a new business. The rest are bank managers. |

1 Look at the products advertised below.

1 What is unusual about each product?
2 Which one interests you most?

2 Read your instructions and prepare for a financial meeting.

BUSINESS PEOPLE: Plan a small business. Use the form below. Think about:

- the product
- the money you need
- the employees
- the advertising
- the market

BANK MANAGERS: You can only give money for one new product. Look at the form below. Prepare other questions to ask to help you decide who's going to get the money. Think about:

- their product
- the money they need
- their employees
- the advertising
- the market

3 As you discuss, make suggestions like this:

| Let's | *make* a video for learning English. |
| Why don't we | *ask* about their business experience? |

4 Each bank manager, see each group of business people in turn. Which group should get the bank loan?

HAMSTER HOTEL ★★★★★

When you go away, GIVE YOUR PETS A BREAK . . . at the HAMSTER HOTEL. Rottweilers NOT welcome . . . £8.50 per night *(including breakfast)*. No children. Bar. Restaurant. Training wheel THE *PERFECT* RODENT RETREAT

GET TO WORK QUICKER!

£6.99 + 25p p+p

SPRING SHOES

Halve your TRAVELLING TIME to the office! Works on all kinds of ROADS and PAVEMENTS. Crash helmet extra. ★★★★ 10 DAY MONEYBACK TRIAL OFFER ★

CUT YOUR DRINKING BY ½ WITH A ½ PINT GLASS

Seen from the front it looks like a full pint. Lose weight and feel better. *Send £2.99 + 26p P&P.* DEPT 69

she/nat west
small business
survey

1. What type of business do you plan to have?

2. Give a brief description of your product.
_____
_____
_____
_____
_____
_____
_____
_____

3. How many people are you going to employ:

a) full-time?
_____

b) part-time?
_____

4. Which of the following do you think you need to be to set up your own business and which do you think you are?

	You need to be	You are
patient		
punctual		
organised		
fair		
creative		
friendly		
clever		
understanding		
fit		
ambitious		

From She

Language review 4

1 Verbs: *should/have to/don't have to* + verb

Use these auxiliary verbs with main verbs to express degrees of obligation.

She *has to* work hard all week. (necessary)
She *doesn't have to* work on Saturdays. (not necessary)
She *should* rest at the weekend. (a good idea)

a Complete these sentences with *should/have to/ don't have to*.

Example: I . . . send Rose a card. It's her birthday on Friday.
I *should* send Rose a card. It's her birthday on Friday.

1 You . . . do the homework tonight. The teacher isn't here tomorrow.
2 You don't look very well. You . . . go to bed.
3 He . . . come to the party if he doesn't want to. He can stay at home.
4 A: Why . . . you . . . go now?
　B: Because I promised I would be home early tonight.
5 If you want my advice, you . . . talk to your parents about it.
6 He . . . finish those reports by 5.00 pm. His boss said it was urgent.
7 I . . . wear a suit to work, but I usually do.

2 Possessive pronouns

Use possessive pronouns so you don't have to repeat the noun.

Possessive adjectives	Possessive pronouns
It's *my* car.	It's *mine*.
It's *your* car.	It's *yours*.
It's *her* car.	It's *hers*.
It's *his* car.	It's *his*.
It's *our* car.	It's *ours*.
It's *their* car.	It's *theirs*.

b What is the person saying each time? Whose is the cat?

3 *Let's . . ./Why don't we . . .?* + verb

For making suggestions that include the speaker.

- **Suggestion**

Let's	go/see/buy/do/eat/make/talk. . .
Why don't we	go/see/buy/do/eat/make/talk. . .?

- **Response**

	OK.
Yes,	that's a good idea.
	fine.
No,	I don't really want to.

c Make suggestions using *Let's . . ./Why don't we . . .?*

Example: A: I'm hungry.
　　　　　B: *Why don't we* go for an Indian meal?

1 A: I'm bored.
　B: Me too . . .
2 A: I'm thirsty.
　B: OK . . .
3 A: We should practise our English.
　B: . . .
4 A: We both need some new shoes.
　B: . . .
5 A: I need some exercise.
　B: . . .

ag ... funding for a new-lo... ...oo.   any more money in its present   ... ...ellamy, ... botanist,   ha... ... ...he zoo this summer   s...

Europe's best and worst!

THE MOST COMPREHENSIVE LIFESTYLE survey of 12 EC countries shows that Britain is second only to Italy in TV ownership - 98 per cent, as opposed to 99 per cent.

BRITAIN
Sweet - toothed Britons consume the most sugar and instant coffee in the EC. The British have the most expensive housing and read the most newspapers. They are also the most ignorant about the EC - for example only one in five knew how many members the EC has.

GERMANY
The health-conscious Germans visit their doctors more than any other Europeans, and also have the most accidents at work. They consume the most beer in the EC, have the most cars, and have more public libraries and museums.

PORTUGAL
The Portuguese have the warmest climate in Europe, the most illiterates, and the longest school holidays. They have the most road accidents, and consume the most rice and fish. They also have the greatest number of policemen per head of population.

IRELAND
The Irish are the most religious Europeans, have the largest families and spend the largest proportion of household budgets on food. They consume the most potatoes in Europe and have the most pet dogs.

SPAIN
The Spanish have Europe's highest rate of unemployment, the most doctors, and eat the most poultry. They watch the most TV, and go on strike more than any other EC workforce.

BELGIUM
The Belgians have the most pharmacists in Europe, the largest number of single-parent families, the most pet cats and the most young unemployed. They also have the highest number of homes linked up to cable TV.

HOLLAND
The Dutch produce the most garbage, their men have the highest life expectancy in the EC, they eat the most citrus fruit, and say they are more satisfied with life than any other Europeans. They buy the most compact discs and own the most boats.

LUXEMBOURG
The tiny principality has the most foreign workers and the most official languages (three). They have the largest proportion of centrally heated homes, and the most washing machines and dish washers.

ITALY
The Italians have the highest rainfall in the EC (in joint first place with the UK). They have the most Catholics, pay the most tax on fuel, and have the most young people still living with their parents. Italy has more TV stations than any other EC country and the lowest fertility rate.

FRANCE
The French drink the most wine in the EC, use the most nuclear power, and their women live the longest. They have the highest number of AIDS cases, and spend the most on health care.

GREECE
Greece has the most islands in the EC, the longest military service and the highest rate of inflation. It has the most smokers, and also consumes the most fruit and vegetables, cheese and mutton.

DENMARK
The Danes pay the most tax in the EC, which may explain why they also have the most suicides. They have the most Protestants, the highest divorce rate and the most illegitimate births.

Pri... spe... end... par... run... line... sin... 'Sc... w... c:... b... ti... la... d... tha... wh... for... yea... Th... sta... Jul... na... per... ...

From *Today*

---

1 Across cultures: lifestyles

> **Revises**
> Vocabulary: Nationalities; countries; languages; transport
> Grammar: Superlatives; Past Simple

1 Look at the article above quickly and answer these questions.

1 Which nationalities is the article about?
2 Which languages do they speak in the countries mentioned?
3 What do you think? What subjects will they mention in the article?

2 Read the questions below. Which subjects in these questions did you think of?

Which country in Europe has:

a) the most expensive housing?
b) the highest life expectancy for men?
c) the highest life expectancy for women?
d) the longest military service?
e) the greatest number of divorces?
f) the most official languages?

g) the warmest climate?
h) the most TV stations?
i) the most pet cats?
j) the most strikes?
k) the largest families?
l) the most cars?

3 Now read the article and answer these questions.

4 Read the article again. What other information did you learn which surprised you?

5 Work with two other students.

1 Name three countries not mentioned in the text.
2 Write a sentence about each one. Say what you think is most special about that country.

6 Say when you last went to any of the countries mentioned. How did you travel there?

2 Thinking about learning: strategies

1 Look at the article again. Find letters/words/ phrases that:

a) describe people who like eating sweet things (Britain).
b) mean a*ccommodation* (Britain).
c) stand for the *European Community* (Britain).
d) describe people who think a lot about how well they are (Germany).
e) mean *to eat/drink* (Germany).
f) describe people who can't read or write (Portugal).
g) describe an animal kept by a family (Ireland).
h) mean *to refuse to work* (Spain).
i) describe families with only one parent (Belgium).
j) describe people who can't find a job (Belgium).
k) mean *a machine for doing the washing up* (Luxembourg).
l) mean *the amount of rain* (Italy).
m) mean *someone who smokes* (Greece).
n) mean *to be born outside of marriage* (Denmark).

2 Work with another student. Which of the following things helped you do the last exercise? Match each letter above to a number below.

Example: a) – 2

1 the beginning or the end of the word, eg. *un-, il-, -ment, -er*
2 the parts of a compound word, eg. *sun + glasses = sunglasses*
3 a word that looks like a word in your/another language, eg. *taxi*
4 the rest of the sentence, eg. She was very hungry so she . . . an apple (*ate*)
5 the initials of a word eg. *BBC* for *British Broadcasting Corporation*

3 Reorder the words in these sentences and make questions to ask about new language in English. (X is the unknown word.)

Example: mean does what X? – What does X mean?

1 say I can X?
2 English for what is the X?
3 you spell how do that?
4 pronounce how you do word this?
5 that again you can please say?
6 this what called is English in?
7 please slowly say more you can that?

4 Now write the questions in the correct column.

Questions with auxiliary *do*	Inverted questions

5 Work with other students. Find out the names of classroom objects you don't know. Do you know the names of all the objects on this page?

Example: A: What is this called in English?
B: A ruler.
A: How do you spell that?
B: R-U-L-E-R.

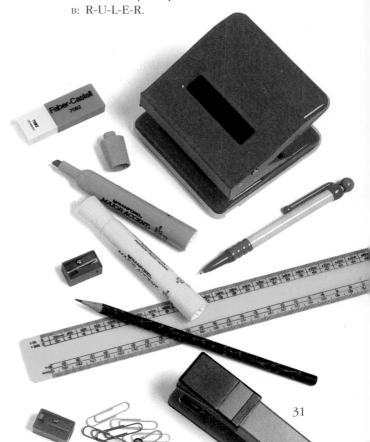

3 Listen again. Which of these expressions do they use exactly?

a) I really liked seeing Paula last week.
b) She used to have problems with . . .
c) Things are worse now.
d) What would you like?
e) I can't remember.
f) I'll have the minestrone soup . . .
g) What is this, exactly?
h) That sounds nice. I'm going to have that.
i) I'll have the soup . . .
j) A bottle of house red, please.

4 Listen again and look at the expressions above. Change the expressions that are different and complete the incomplete sentences.

5 Order your meal from this English menu. If necessary, ask the waiter/waitress about dishes, like this:

CUSTOMER: Excuse me. What is steak and kidney pie exactly?

WAITER: Well, it's a typical English dish . . .

3 Language in context: eating out

Revises
Vocabulary: Restaurants; nationalities
Grammar: *Should/have to/don't have to; going to* vs *will*

1 Talk to other students. What do you think? When you invite a new friend to a restaurant for the first time should you:

• reserve a table before you go?
• arrive before she/he does?
• check if she/he is a vegetarian?
• choose what to drink with the meal?
• share the bill?
• drive her/him home?

2 ▣ Listen to the couple above, ordering a meal in a restaurant. Answer these questions.
1 What type of food do they want?
2 Which of these things do they mention:
   a friend/their boss/the service/the wine/the bill?
3 Who else speaks?

PORTERS

STARTERS

PRAWN COCKTAIL

FRESH TOMATO SOUP

FARMHOUSE PATE

MAIN COURSES
*All served with roast or new potatoes
and a selection of fresh vegetables,
or green salad*

STEAK AND KIDNEY PIE

LANCASHIRE HOT-POT

ROAST BEEF AND YORKSHIRE PUDDING

CHICKEN AND MUSHROOM PIE

SWEETS

BREAD AND BUTTER PUDDING

APPLE CRUMBLE AND CUSTARD

FRESH FRUIT SALAD AND CREAM

6 Work with another student. Look at the advertisements for London restaurants on this page and decide which restaurant is best for these people. Use each restaurant once only.

a) A family who want to celebrate a birthday after going to the theatre which finishes at 11.15 pm.
b) Two accountants who want a business lunch but are bored with European food.
c) A group of sixteen-year-olds on a shopping spree.
d) A doctor who particularly loves French and Italian food. She likes listening to live music.
e) A couple going out for the first time together. They want a romantic evening. One of them is a vegetarian.
f) Very hungry students who haven't eaten all day and are on a limited budget.

7 In groups, discuss which restaurant you'd like to go to together.

1 Which type of food would you like to eat?
2 Which day and time can you all go?
3 Where will you meet?
4 What will you do afterwards?

8 Tell other groups what you are going to do.

Check What You Know!
Now turn to page 127 and complete Check What You Know 1.

6 | Obsessions

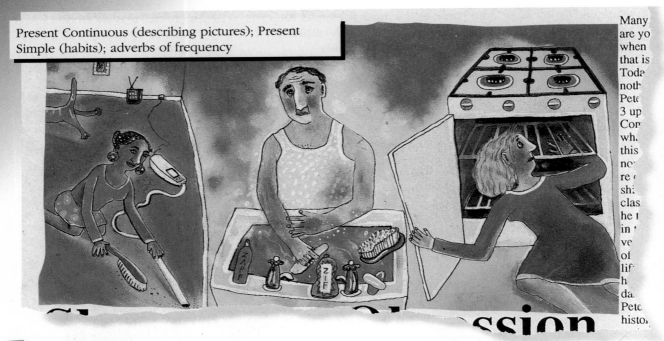

1 Preparation

1 **Describe the picture above. What are the people doing?**

2 **Read about people's habits in the newspaper extracts and discuss these questions with another student.**

1 What do you think of this behaviour?

2 Which is usual? Which is obsessive?

3 What makes it obsessive?

3 **Ask your partner about each habit. Does she/he do any of these things?**

Example: Do you make lists of things to do?

Yes, always.

Yes, sometimes.

No, never.

4 **Tell your partner about a habit you used to have but don't have any more.**

Example: I used to smoke, but I don't any more.

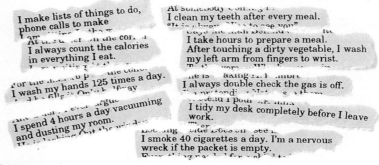

I make lists of things to do, phone calls to make

At somebody coming in
I clean my teeth after every meal.
"It is always time to see you"

I always count the calories in everything I eat.

I take hours to prepare a meal.
After touching a dirty vegetable, I wash my left arm from fingers to wrist.

I wash my hands 125 times a day.

I always double check the gas is off.

I spend 4 hours a day vacuuming and dusting my room.

I tidy my desk completely before I leave work.

I smoke 40 cigarettes a day. I'm a nervous wreck if the packet is empty.

2 Speaking

1 **Add more questions to this questionnaire. Find out how often people do things.**

How often:	Very often	Quite often	Occasionally	Never
do you watch TV?				
do you go out with friends?				
do you go to the opera?				
. . . ?				
. . . ?				
. . . ?				

2 **Ask another student the questions and note her/his answers.**

Writing

> She quite *often* goes to the cinema.
> She goes to the cinema quite *often*.
> She *never* goes to the cinema.

1 Look at the examples above and answer these questions about the adverbs *often* and *never*.

1 Which can go before the verb?
2 Which can't go at the end of the sentence?

2 Look at the adverbs below. What do you think? Which other adverb can't go at the end of the sentence?

100% ◄――――――――――――――► 0%
always   often   sometimes   occasionally   never

3 Use the information from the questionnaire to write sentences about your partner's habits.

Example: Begonia often watches TV. She quite
often goes out with friends, but she
never goes to the opera.

3 Grammar

Present Simple vs Present Continuous

> a) She is smoking.
> b) She smokes 20 cigarettes a day.

1 Look at the sentences above and answer these questions.

1 Which sentence describes her habit, a) or b)?
2 Which sentence describes her action at the present moment, a) or b)?

2 Write these forms in the correct column below.

Is she smoking?   Yes, she does.
No, she isn't.   She isn't smoking a cigar.
Does she smoke?   She doesn't smoke cigars.
Yes, she is.   No, she doesn't.

Present Continuous	Present Simple
She is smoking.	She smokes 20 cigarettes a day.

4 Pronunciation: contrastive stress

1 🔊 Listen. Which words have got main stress in the dialogue below?

A: Are you wearing my <u>jacket</u>?
B: No, it's my jacket, not your jacket.
A: Well, it looks like my jacket.
B: But it isn't your jacket. It's blue, not black.

2 Practise the dialogue with another student. Stress the contrasted words.

3 Look at the picture of Jan's room below with another student. What can you say about her from her room? Use these verbs.

Example: She plays tennis.

listen   play   drink   smoke
read   watch   wear   like

4 Find out what Jan is doing now.

STUDENT A: Look at the picture on page 124.
Answer Student B's questions and say
what Jan is doing now.

STUDENT B: Look at the picture on this page. Use
the ideas below to make questions in
the Present Continuous.

sit at/desk?   read/book?
listen/a CD?   wear/a black T-shirt?
drink/coffee?   wear/dark blue jeans?

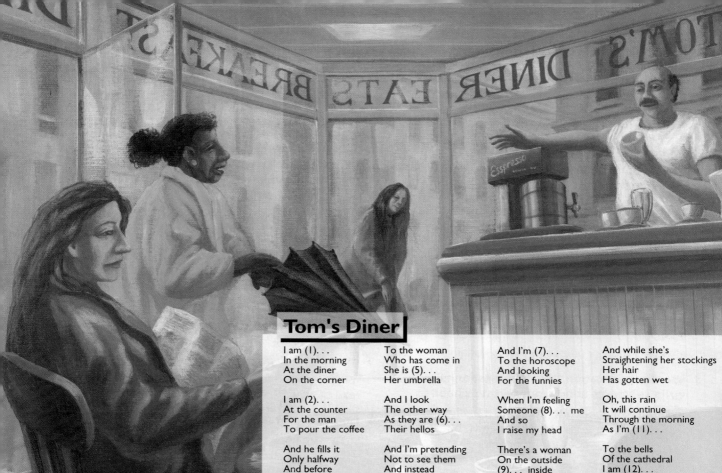

Tom's Diner

I am (1). . .
In the morning
At the diner
On the corner

I am (2). . .
At the counter
For the man
To pour the coffee

And he fills it
Only halfway
And before
I even argue

He is (3). . .
Out the window
At somebody
(4). . . in

"It is always
Nice to see you"
Says the man
Behind the counter

To the woman
Who has come in
She is (5). . .
Her umbrella

And I look
The other way
As they are (6). . .
Their hellos

And I'm pretending
Not to see them
And instead
I pour the milk

I open
Up the paper
There's a story
Of an actor

Who had died
While he was drinking
It was no one
I had heard of

And I'm (7). . .
To the horoscope
And looking
For the funnies

When I'm feeling
Someone (8). . . me
And so
I raise my head

There's a woman
On the outside
(9). . . inside
Does she see me?

No she does not
Really see me
Cause she sees
Her own reflection

And I'm (10). . .
Not to notice
That she's hitching
Up her skirt

And while she's
Straightening her stockings
Her hair
Has gotten wet

Oh, this rain
It will continue
Through the morning
As I'm (11). . .

To the bells
Of the cathedral
I am (12). . .
Of your voice

And of the midnight picnic
Once upon a time
Before the rain began

And I finish up my coffee
And it's time to catch the tra

Suzanne Vega 1982

5 Listening

1 Before you listen, describe what you can see in the picture above with another student.

2 Now write six sentences describing what is happening in the picture.

Example: A young woman is sitting at a table.

3 Tell the class your sentences. Add other students' sentences to your list.

4 📼 Close your books. Listen to the song and answer these questions.

   1 Which of your sentences are referred to in the song?

   2 Who in the picture is singing the song?

5 Look at the words of the song with your partner. Complete each gap with one of these verbs in the correct form.

kiss   look   sit   try   wait   shake
turn   listen   watch   think   come   look

6 Listen again. Were you correct?

7 Read the words again and answer these questions.

   1 What is the singer really thinking about?

   2 How does she feel?

Sports (football); *don't mind + -ing* form

6 Reading

1 Before you read, answer these questions with other students.

1 How many sports can you name between you?
2 How many players are there in a football *team?*
3 What is the difference between a football *ground* and a football *match?* Which is the game? Which is the place?
4 What is the difference between *a home* and *an away* match?
5 What is the advantage of buying *a season ticket?* When is *the football season?*
6 What is another word for *football?*
7 What do football *supporters* do? When do they *cheer?*

2 Read the article and find this information about Glenys.

name   age   sex   team   other sporting interests

3 Read the article again and decide if these statements are true (T) or false (F).

Example: Glenys only sees Swansea City play at home. – F.

1 Glenys' parents used to babysit for her.
2 Her son never went to football matches with her.
3 Glenys doesn't know anyone who likes going to football matches as much as she does.
4 Glenys thinks it's expensive to follow her team.
5 Glenys goes to matches by bus.
6 Glenys does a lot of other social activities.
7 Glenys likes football and cricket equally.

Grammar: *don't mind + -ing* form

> /n/   /n/ /n/   /ŋ/   /ŋ/
> Glenys *doesn't mind* travell*ing* a long way to see Swansea City.

1 Look at the sentence above. Is it or isn't it a problem for Glenys?

2 Repeat the sentence, making sure you don't add a /g/ to the /ŋ/ sounds.

3 Put these things in the correct column for Glenys.

a) travelling by coach
b) leaving her son with her parents
c) seeing Swansea play
d) staying in cheap hotels
e) having no social life
f) watching cricket
g) watching football
h) missing a match

She enjoys	She doesn't mind	She hates

4 Tell another student how you feel about:

a) staying at home on Saturday night.
b) looking after young children.
c) spending holidays with the family.
d) going to parties.
e) going to the hairdresser's.
f) shopping for clothes.
g) doing the washing up.
h) complaining in a shop.

From *Living*

FOOTBALL FANATICISM

1 Soccer fanatic Glenys Grenfell is Swansea City football team's number one supporter. 59-year-old Glenys has seen more than 2000
5 matches and will travel anywhere in Britain to see her team in action. Last year she saw the 'Swans' play at every football ground in Britain.
Glenys is so single-minded about
10 football she refuses to let anything stand in the way of her Saturday afternoon match - even motherhood! Two weeks after her son David was born in 1959, Glenys was back to
15 cheer the team on - while her parents were at home babysitting! "They looked after David until he was about seven and then I started taking him to matches with me. He
20 came with me occasionally up until three years ago but he didn't enjoy it as much as me. In fact no-one I know does. My family and friends all think I'm a bit crazy!"
25 She admits it is a costly hobby, especially going to away matches, because she prefers to drive herself rather than travel on the supporters' bus as she gets sick on coaches.
30 "My season ticket costs £120 a year but that's only for home games. I go to away matches two or three times a month and spend about £20 each time on petrol, entrance fees
35 and food. If the match is far away I prefer to drive up the night before and stay in an inexpensive hotel."
So how does she afford it? "I don't drink or smoke and rarely go
40 out socially. I can't remember the last time I went to the cinema or theatre," she explains. The football season starts in August and ends in early May. But Glenys certainly
45 doesn't stop in the summer months. Instead she turns her attention to her other passion - cricket. "I love cricket although not as much as soccer. I start watching in April but
50 only if there's no football. Some people would say I'm too obsessive about football but I don't agree. It's just an important part of my life. ■

ENGLISH IN ACTION

Prepare a talk about something that particularly interests you.

1 **Work with other students. Look at the photographs of hobbies on this page.**

1 Which can you name?
2 Have you ever done any of these things?

2 🔲 **Listen to someone talking about one of these hobbies. Which hobby is he talking about? What does he like about it?**

3 **Think of a subject you are very interested in. Prepare to give a short talk to the class.**

1 Make notes about what you are going to say.
2 Check you know the necessary vocabulary.
3 Use pictures, photographs and/or objects to tell the class about your subject. Think about:

   • when/how this interest began.
   • how often you do it.
   • what you enjoy most about it.

Give your talk.

4 **Listen to other students. Ask them questions to get more information.**

Language review 6

1 Adverbs of frequency

Adverbs of frequency answer the question *How often . . .?*

100%	always
	usually
	often
	sometimes
	occasionally
0%	never

In sentences, *always* and *never* go before the verb.
She *always/never* reads before she goes to sleep.

The other adverbs go before the verb or at the beginning/end of the sentence.
Sometimes she goes to the theatre.
She *sometimes* goes to the theatre.
She goes to the theatre *sometimes*.

a In five of these sentences the word order is definitely wrong. Rewrite them in the correct order.
1 I visit sometimes friends at the weekend.
2 I quite often do my homework in the morning.
3 I play golf on Saturday afternoons always.
4 I occasionally watch rugby on TV.
5 Never I do the shopping during the week.
6 I take my children always to the park on Sundays.
7 I don't go swimming very often.
8 We go usually to the cinema on Fridays.
9 I never see him these days.
10 Sometimes he phones after work.

2 Verbs: Present Simple vs Present Continuous

Present Simple is used for present habits.
(For Present Simple forms, see Unit 0 on page 5).

Present Continuous is used to talk about actions happening at the present moment.
She smokes but she isn't smoking at the moment. She's eating.

- **Present Continuous**

Positive/Negative

I	am	
You/We/They	are	(not) eat*ing*.
She/He/It	is	

Question

Am	I	
Are	you/we/they	eat*ing*?
Is	she/he/it	

b Complete these sentences, using the verb in brackets in the Present Simple or Present Continuous form.
Example: (go) He . . . to work at 8 o'clock every day.
He goes to work at 8 o'clock every day.
1 (have) I'm sorry, he . . . a shower at the moment.
2 (play) She . . . football on Thursday evenings.
3 (paint) I can't answer the door, I . . . the bathroom ceiling.
4 (clean) I . . . the car most Sundays.
5 (visit) They often . . . their grandchildren in Australia but it's very expensive to go.
6 (do) It is very quiet because the children . . . their homework.

c Correct the mistakes in these dialogues.
1 A: Excuse me, are you speaking English?
   B: Yes, I do, a little. Can I help?
2 A: Hi! Where are you?
   B: I'm in the living room. I watch TV.

3 *Don't mind + -ing* form

Use *don't mind + -ing* to talk about something generally considered negative, but not a problem to the speaker.

| + | OK | − |
| like | don't mind | don't like |

I don't mind doing housework. I don't like it particularly but it's not a problem.

d Rewrite these sentences, using *don't mind* or *don't like*.
Example: It's not that bad going to work by train.
I don't mind going to work by train.
1 She's quite happy to do the washing-up.
2 It is very difficult for him to share his office with people who smoke.
3 I'm going home now. I want to miss the rush hour.
4 I'm happy to work late if it's necessary.

7 Spotlight

1 Preparation

1 Look at the travel souvenirs on this page with another student. What do you think?

1 Where has their owner been?
2 What makes you think this?

Example: I think she's been to Japan because she's got a Japanese kimono.

2 Ask your partner about these and other countries.

Example: Have you ever been to . . .?

> Yes, once/twice/three times.

> Yes, lots of times.

> No, never.

3 Complete these questions with interesting things you want to know about other students' experiences.

1 Have you (ever) seen . . .?
2 Have you (ever) heard . . .?
3 Have you (ever) tasted . . .?
4 Have you (ever) met . . .?
5 Have you (ever) visited . . .?

4 Ask your questions. How many people have/haven't done these things?

> **NB** Present Perfect of *have*
>
>   1   2
> Have you ever had Chinese food?
>
> a) Which is the main verb, 1 or 2?
> b) Which is the auxiliary for forming the Present Perfect?

2 Grammar: Present Perfect vs Past Simple

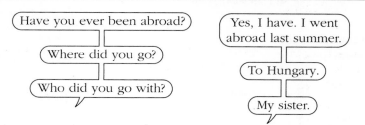

> Have you ever been abroad?
>
> Where did you go?
>
> Who did you go with?

> Yes, I have. I went abroad last summer.
>
> To Hungary.
>
> My sister.

1 Look at the questions above.

1 Which question/s are in the Past Simple? Which is/are in the Present Perfect?
2 Which form refers to specific time/detail?
3 Which form refers to general experience?
4 How do you form the Present Perfect? How do you make the negative and question form?

2 Complete this chart. What do you notice about the Past Simple and past participle of *meet*, *hear*, *taste* and *visit*?

Present	Past Simple	Past participle
go	went	been/gone
see	. . .	seen
do	did	. . .
eat	. . .	eaten
meet	met	. . .
hear	heard	. . .
taste	. . .	. . .
visit	. . .	. . .

Pronunciation

> How many countries have you been to?

1 📼 **Listen and repeat the question above.**

1 Which word has got main information and stress?
2 How do you pronounce *have*? How do you pronounce *been*?

2 **Make more questions from the words below. Use the Present Perfect or the Past Simple.**

1 How many jobs/had?
  How many schools/go to?
  When/start/present job or school?
2 What types of food/eaten?
  (eg. Indian, Italian, etc.)
  When/last eat out?
  Where . . . ?
  What . . . ?
3 . . . see/any of these films?
  When/see them?
  What/think of them?

  Silence of the Lambs
  Batman
  Gone with the Wind
  Dances with Wolves
  Cyrano de Bergerac

3 **Now ask other students your questions to find out:**

1 who has had the most jobs/ been to the most schools.
2 who has eaten the greatest variety of food.
3 who has seen the most films on the list.

3 Listening

1 📼 **Listen to people as they come out of the cinema. What did they think about the film they saw? Tick the correct column.**

	couldn't stand	didn't like	quite liked	liked	loved
Person 1					
Person 2					
Person 3					
Person 4					
Person 5					

2 **Listen again. Which of these adjectives does each person use?**

Example: Person 1 – frightening

frightening exciting boring depressing
disgusting disappointing amusing interesting

3 **Listen again and mark the stress on each word. How many syllables has each word got?**

        1   2
Example: 'frightening

4 **Work with another student. Group the adjectives under these headings.**

Positive	Negative

4 Grammar: Present Perfect (recent past)

> These people *have* just *been* to the cinema.

1 **Look at the sentence above and answer these questions.**

1 Is the Present Perfect used here to describe what happened a long time ago or recently?
2 Which word means *a short time ago*?

2 **Use information from Exercise 3 Listening above. Tell another student about the film each cinema-goer has just seen.**

Example: The first person has (just) seen a frightening film.

3 **Ask your partner about films she/he has seen recently.**

Example: A: Have you seen any good films recently?
            B: Yes, *Gandhi*.
            A: What was it like?

Pronunciation: /æ/ vs /ʌ/

1 Complete the chart.

1 Present	2 Past Simple	3 Past participle
. . .	swam	swum
. . .	ran	run
. . .	drank	drunk
. . .	rang	rung
. . .	began	begun
. . .	sang	sung

2 ▣ Listen to the difference in pronunciation between *swam* /swæm/ and *swum* /swʌm/.

3 ▣ Now listen to some of the verbs above. Which column does each one come from, 2 or 3?

4 Test another student in the same way.

5 Work with another student. Use one of the verbs above to describe each film still. What has just happened?

Example: 1 – She has (just) swum across the pool.

5 Vocabulary: *-ed*/*-ing* adjectives

1 Find two forms of each adjective in the film reviews below and answer these questions.

1 Which ending describes how people feel, *-ing* or *-ed*?
2 Which ending describes what makes them feel this, *-ing* or *-ed*?

2 Work with another student. Complete these unfinished reviews with one of these adjectives.

frightened/frightening   depressed/depressing
amused/amusing   disgusted/disgusting
disappointed/disappointing

1 Really . . .! I laughed till I cried!
2 Don't be . . . Book your tickets early!
3 Horrific! Very . . . You won't sleep for a week!
4 A very . . . film. Everybody dies or lives a life of misery.
5 . . . parents want violent film banned.

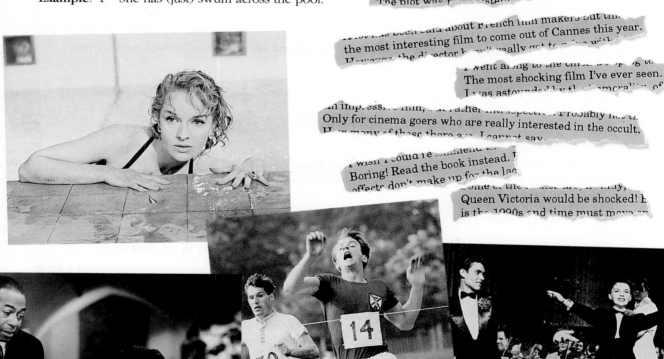

I was bored from beginning to end.
The plot was non existent . . .

. . . has been said about French film makers but this is the most interesting film to come out of Cannes this year.
However, the director . . . 't really get to . . .

. . . went along to the cinema . . .
The most shocking film I've ever seen.
I was astounded by the immorality of . . .

. . . an impressive film, . . . rather introspective . . . Probably not . .
Only for cinema goers who are really interested in the occult.
How many of these there are I cannot say.

I wish I could re . . .
Boring! Read the book instead. . .
effects don't make up for the lac . . .

. . . some of the . . . but are, if . . . ly,
Queen Victoria would be shocked! E . .
is the 1990s and time must move on . .

Scandal

FILM: PREVIEW

FILM

From March to June 1963, Britain was rocked by scandal. The film shows how Dr Stephen Ward met seventeen-year-old showgirl Christine Keeler. It tells how, under his influence, she began her relationship with the government minister, John Profumo. What started as an **amused/amusing** little affair soon became a **shocked/shocking** political scandal; Christine Keeler was sleeping with other members of high society. Among them was Ivanov, a Russian diplomatic attaché. Did she pass on government secrets? Did Ward live off immoral earnings?

Depressed/depressing and **frightened/frightening** for his social position, Ward committed suicide. Christine Keeler went to prison and a government minister lost his job. The British public were **disgusted/disgusting** by the lies and hypocrisy but never **bored/boring** by the scandal. Many people think it contributed to the fall of the Conservative Government in 1964.

All in all, an **excited/exciting** film. It raises **interested/interesting** questions long after the scandal itself. It is well acted and should not be missed!

6 Reading

1 Before you read the review of the film *Scandal*, what does the title mean? What different types of scandal are there?

2 Read the review. Is it negative or positive?

1 What was the scandal?
2 Where/When did it happen?
3 Who were the people in the scandal?
4 What happened to them?
5 What was the political effect?

3 Work with another student. Choose the correct adjectives in the text.

7 Writing

1 Complete this table.

Subject pronouns		Possessive adjectives		Object pronouns
I		my		me.
You		. . .		you.
She		her		. . .
He	passed	. . .	secrets to	him.
It		. . .		it.
We		our		. . .
You		your		. . .
They		. . .		them.

2 Work with another student. Find the pronouns and possessive adjectives in the review of *Scandal*. Who/What do they refer to?

3 Write a short review of a book, a film, or a play you have seen. Use pronouns and possessive adjectives where you can.

1 What is the basic story?
2 Who are the important characters?
3 What did you think of it?

ENGLISH IN ACTION

PLAZA   A LUXURY CINEMA IN THE HEART OF LONDON   PLAZA

Sep. Progs. Daily: 12.15, 2.25, 4.55, 6.45, 8.55 Late shows Fri. and Sat. 11.30pm

Sep. Progs. Daily: 12.30 3.10, 5.50, 8.30 Late Shows Fri. And Sat. 11.20pm

Sep. Progs Daily: 1.00, 3.00, 5.00, 7.00, 9.00 Late Shows Fri. and Sat. 11.15pm

Sep. Progs. Daily: 12.05, 2.25, 4.45, 7.05, 9.30 Late shows Fri. and Sat. 11.50pm

Fri. and Sat. Only: 1.00, 6.30, 10.30 Sun. to Thurs: 12.00, 4.00, 8.00

Sep. Progs. Daily: 1.00, 3.15, 6.00, 8.30 Late Shows Fri. and Sat. 11.00pm

Plan an evening at the cinema with a group from your class.

1 Read the film advertisement with another student. Which of these types of film can't you see? Which is:

a) a love story?   e) a science fiction film?
b) a western?   f) a cartoon?
c) a horror film?   g) a comedy?
d) a thriller?

2 🖳 Listen and check your answers. Where's the stress on each type of film?

3 Tell your partner the type of film you like best. Decide which film above you would both most like to see.

1 Do you know who is in it?
2 Where is it on?
3 What time is it on?

4 In groups, decide which film to see together. Try to persuade your group to go to the film *you* want to see. Make suggestions, like this:

Let's	*go* to	*Casablanca.*
Why don't we	*see*	a horror film?

What about	go*ing* to	*Casablanca?*
How about	see*ing*	a horror film?

5 Tell other groups which film you have decided to see. Can you persuade other students to join your group?

44

Language review 7

1 Verbs

- **Present Perfect and Past Simple**

Use Present Perfect to talk about general experience.
Use Past Simple to talk about specific time/detail.

Present Perfect		Past Simple
I *have* I've	*been* to Japan.	I *went* to Japan last year.
She *has* She's	*been* to India.	She *went* by plane.

- **Present Perfect (recent past)**

You can use Present Perfect +/– *just* to talk about recent past events.

Positive

I/You/We/They	*have*	(just) *been* to the cinema.
She/he/it	*has*	

Negative

I/You/We/They	*have*	not (just) *been* to the cinema.
She/He/It	*has*	

Question

Have	I/you/we/they	(just) *been* to the cinema?
Has	she/he/it	

a Complete this job interview between an Interviewer (I) and a Candidate (C). Put the verbs in brackets in the Present Perfect or Past Simple.

I: So, tell me a little about the things you . . . (do).
C: Well, I . . . (study) French and German at university. Then, I . . . (teach) in secondary school for a few years.
I: . . . you (enjoy) teaching?
C: No, not really. I . . . (not like) the discipline problems. So, I . . . (start) working for a large drug company.
I: . . . you (work) abroad at all?
C: Yes, well about three years ago I . . . (get) a job in France, selling advertising space for a science magazine.
I: . . . you (go) anywhere else?
C: Yes, I . . . (work) in Germany in 1990.
I: Oh really? What . . . (do) there?

b Look at the pictures. What has just happened in each picture?

2 Adjectives ending in *-ed* and *-ing*

We feel . . . *-ed*	because something is . . . *-ing.*
bored	boring
interested	interesting
shocked	shocking
frightened	frightening
amused	amusing
disappointed	disappointing
depressed	depressing
disgusted	disgusting

c Choose the correct adjective in these sentences.

1 Are you interesting/interested in photography?
2 Do you get embarrassing/embarrassed easily?
3 The tennis match was very exciting/excited.
4 When I was a child, I was frightening/frightened of dogs.
5 The holiday was a shocking/shocked waste of money.
6 Don't read that. It's really boring/bored.
7 I was disappointing/disappointed by my exam results.

3 Possessive adjectives and object pronouns

Possessive adjectives	Object pronouns
my	me
your	you
her	her
his	him
its	it
our	us
their	them

d Complete the gaps in this story with a possessive adjective or an object pronoun.

I took . . . car round to my sister's house last night. She wasn't at home but . . . husband was. He asked . . . to wait because she was on . . . way home. I started looking at . . . photo albums and found all the old photos of . . . as children with . . . parents. There were also some photos of our parents before we were born. There was a lovely one of . . . with . . . dog, Bess.

Movie time

1 Work with other students. Plan a film together.

2 Look at the photographs and put them in order to make your film. (Different orders are possible.)

3 What do you think? What has just happened in each photograph? What is going to happen next?

4 Write the script for your film. Use your dictionary if you need vocabulary.

5 Show the script to your teacher. Correct it where necessary.

6 Take one part each and learn your words.

7 Watch or read the script of other students' films. Which film do you like best?

8 Consequences

So vs because

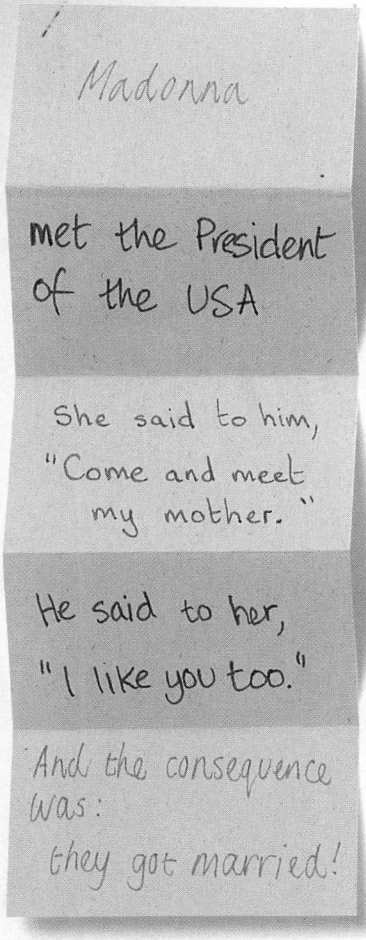

met
Luciano Pavarotti

She said to him,
"You've got
beautiful teeth."

He said to her,
"I'm never going
to leave you."

And the consequence
was:
Brazil won the
World Cup.

Madonna

met the President
of the USA

She said to him,
"Come and meet
my mother."

He said to her,
"I like you too."

And the consequence
was:
they got married!

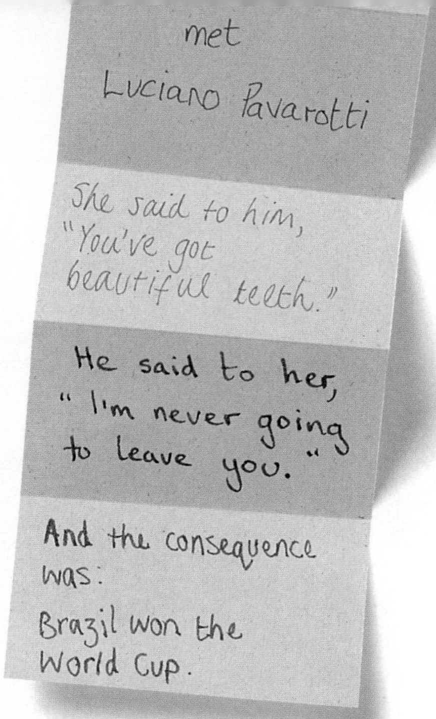

2 Writing: _so vs because_

> They got married _because_ they loved each other.
> They got married _so_ they went on a honeymoon.

1 Look at the examples above and answer these questions.

1 Which word introduces the reason for the marriage, _so_ or _because_?
2 Which word introduces the result, _so_ or _because_?

2 Work with another student. Write logical sentences from the chart below, using _so_ or _because_ each time. Use each sentence on the left twice, and each sentence on the right once only.

Example: They went to Greece by boat _because_ it was more romantic.
They went to Greece by boat _so_ it took a long time.

They went to Greece by boat		it was the middle of August.
		it was the end of their holiday.
They stayed in a cheap hotel		it took a long time.
		they went to the beach a lot.
It was very hot in Greece	so	it was more romantic.
	because	the room wasn't very comfortable.
They decided to go to a		they didn't have much money.
disco on their last night		they woke up late and
		missed the boat home.

3 Work in groups. Write down a possible reason and result for each of these statements, using _because_ and _so_.

1 More and more people are learning English.
2 Alcoholism is becoming more of a social problem.
3 School standards are getting lower.
4 More and more people have become unemployed.
5 People are living longer.

4 Compare your answers with another group. Which group has got the most interesting reason or result?

1 Preparation

1 Play _Consequences_ with a group of students. Take a piece of paper to write on.

2 🖥 Listen and follow the instructions.

3 Unfold the paper and read the complete story to other students.

4 Listen to other students' stories. Decide which story is the most amusing.

budget.

Get ahead of your time

by IAN BROWN

WHAT WILL people in hundreds of years time think of us and our lifestyle?

To give them clues, more and more time capsules are being buried around the country. The largest time capsule is buried at Castle Howard in Yorkshire. Containing nearly 800 items, it was put there in 1982 to mark the BBC's 60th birthday, and is not to be opened until the year 3982. As well as more than a mile of film of television programmes, the cont - ents include a set of false teeth and a zip fastener.

Heads seek

From *The Daily Mail*

Time trapped in a capsule

les will present his case today

The first modern time capsule was sponsored by the American Westinghouse Company in 1938. They wanted the contents to represent 'a cross-section of our time'. But Dr Brian Durans of the British Museum says any time capsule will mislead future historians. The proof of this is the contents of a space capsule, sent into space never to return. Among the things sent to tell of our existence were compact discs and pictures of a man and a woman. It was enough to convince anyone that Earth was full of perfectly-formed, white, Beatles fans!

From *The Indy*

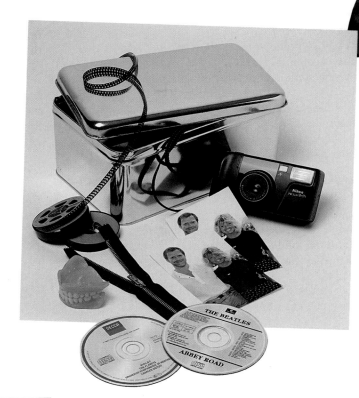

3 Reading

1 Before you read, match these names to the objects in the picture above.

a compact disc   a camera   film
false teeth   a space capsule   a zip
a photograph

2 Read the articles and answer these questions.

1 What is the connection between the objects and the newspaper articles?
2 What is the idea behind a time capsule?

3 Read the articles again and answer these questions.

1 Where is the biggest time capsule buried?
2 How many things are in it?
3 When was it buried?
4 Why was it buried?
5 When will it be opened?

6 When was the first time capsule thought of?
7 Who had the idea?
8 What is the problem for historians?
9 What two things in the time capsule in space are mentioned?
10 What misunderstanding could these things cause?

4 Look at the articles again. Find the underlined words that mean:

a) a possible piece of evidence. (*n.*)
b) to suggest something false. (*v.*)
c) a good selection. (*n.*)
d) this planet. (*n.*)
e) the way we live. (*n.*)
f) things inside something. (*n.*)
g) to persuade. (*v.*)
h) evidence that shows something is true. (*n.*)

If/when + future; *definitely/probably* (word order);
if + present + *will* (first conditional)

4 Grammar: *If/when* + future

> a) *If* they open the space time capsule, they'll
> think we are all 'perfectly formed, white,
> Beatles fans'.
> b) *When* they open the capsule in 3982, they'll
> think we watch a lot of films.

**1 Look at the sentences above and answer
these questions.**

1 Which sentence means they will *definitely* open
the capsule, a) or b)?
2 Which sentence means *perhaps* they will open
it?
3 Are the sentences about the present or the
future?
4 Is the verb after *if/when* in a present or a future
form?

**2 Rearrange these words to make sentences about
the future.**

1 you wait won't are late if for I evening you this
2 lunch hungry you eat later be will don't you if
3 her her I tell I see will when
4 the office finish I it will into I when bring your
report
5 stay refuse if will ask me they to I
6 she problem rings when she you tell will the

**3 Complete these sentences about the future with
if or *when*.**

1 What will you do . . . you get home this
evening?
2 What will you do . . . there's a transport strike
tomorrow?
3 What will you do . . . it rains this weekend?
4 What will you do . . . this course finishes?
5 Where will you live . . . you are old?

**4 ▣ Listen and repeat the completed sentences.
Say the words *what will* and *where will* like this:**

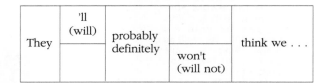

**5 Have short conversations with different
students. Begin each conversation with a
different question from above.**

5 Speaking

**1 Talk to another student. Discuss filling your own
time capsule.**

1 What do you want people in the future to
know about your lifestyle?
2 What will you put in your capsule?
3 When would you like people to open it?

**2 Talk to another pair of students and list the
things they chose. Tell them why you chose the
things you did.**

Example: We chose a pair of jeans because/so . .

**3 Discuss the contents of the other students'
capsule with your partner. What will people in
the future think when they open it? Discuss
what you think, like this:**

They	'll (will)	probably definitely		think we . . .
			won't (will not)	

**4 Now write what you think for the other
students to read, like this:**

If you put jeans in your capsule, they'll think we
only wear jeans.

6 Vocabulary: education

1 **Read these questions. Use your mini-dictionary on page 138 to check the meaning and pronunciation of any new vocabulary.**

1 Did you go to a *state school* or a *private school*?

2 Which of these *subjects* did you study?

a modern language	maths	history
your own language	sciences	Latin
religious education	geography	
physical education	art	

a) Did you study them at *primary* or *secondary school* or in *higher education* (e.g. *university*)?

b) Did you study any other subjects?

3 What are the names of the important *exams* in your country?

a) At what age do you *take* them?

b) What happens if you *fail* them? Can you *retake* them?

c) What difference does it make if you *pass* them?

d) Are the exam *grades* important?

e) Do you get a *certificate*?

f) What *qualifications* do you need to get a good job?

2 **Discuss the questions above with other students.**

NB Word families		
Subject	**Job**	**Adjective**
'art	'artist	ar'tistic
'science	'scientist	scien'tific
'history	hi'storian	hi'storic

Where does the stress go on adjectives ending in *-ic*?

7 Listening

1 🖭 **Listen to this student talking about the exams she is taking in Britain.**

1 Which of the questions in Exercise 6 Vocabulary does she answer?

2 What are her answers?

2 **Listen again. Write what she says will happen:**

a) if she passes her exams.

b) if she fails her exams.

c) when she leaves school in July.

Pronunciation

1st clause	2nd clause
If I pass,	I'll go to university.
I'll go to university,	if I pass.

1 🖭 **Listen to the two sentences above and answer these questions.**

1 Does the speaker's voice go up or down at the end of the 1st clause? Is the sentence finished?

2 Does the speaker's voice go up or down at the end of the 2nd clause? Is the sentence finished?

2 **Practise saying the sentences.**

3 **Find out which students in the class are taking other exams/courses. What will they do:**

a) if they pass the exams?

b) when they finish the course?

ENGLISH IN ACTION

Find out what English exams you can take in your country.

1 Prepare to write a letter to ask for information about exams. Write sentences and questions to include in your letter.

1 Tell them:
   a) what level you are.
   b) what book/course you are studying.
   c) where you are studying.

2 Ask them:
   a) where you can take the different exams.
   b) what level your English needs to be.
   c) for any other information they can give you.
   d) if they have any sample papers for you to see.
   e) how much the exam fees are.

2 Look at these expressions. Which come at the beginning of your letter? Which come at the end?

Yours faithfully,

I am writing to...

Dear Sir / Madam,

Thank you for your help in this matter.

Please send me information about...

Now write your letter.

3 Write your address in the top right-hand-corner, followed by the date.

4 📟 Listen and write the address to send your letter to on the left-hand-side.

Now send your letter.

Language review 8

1 *So* vs *because*

Because introduces a reason.
So introduces a result.
She bought the dress *because* she liked it.
She liked the dress *so* she bought it.

a Finish these sentences to show the meaning of *so/because*.

Example: It was raining so . . . – It was raining *so I took my umbrella with me.*

1 I really didn't like the film because . . .
2 I didn't have enough money to pay the bill so . . .
3 I decided to change my job because . . .
4 I stayed in bed all morning because . . .
5 The party next door was so loud I couldn't sleep so . . .

2 *If* and *when* + future time

If/when + Present Simple expresses future time.

If = perhaps it will happen.
When = it will definitely happen.
I'll phone you *when* he comes home.
I'll phone you *if* he comes home.

b Complete each sentence below with an *if/when* clause.

Example: Perhaps it'll snow. *If it snows*, we won't go out.

1 Paulette will arrive soon. . . ., I'll ask her to phone you.
2 He'll probably feel better tomorrow. . . ., he'll go back to school.
3 The TV programme finishes in half an hour. . . ., we'll have dinner.
4 Perhaps I'll see Mark later. . . ., I'll tell him.

3 *If* + present + *will* (The first conditional)

- **If + Present Simple**

This expresses a possible future condition.

A: Will you take an umbrella?
B: *If* it rains.

- **Will/won't + verb**

This expresses the result of the possible condition.

A: What *will* you do if it rains?
B: I'*ll* take an umbrella.

- **The first conditional**

The first conditional talks about a possible future condition and its result.

If +	Present Simple	+ subject + *will*	+ verb
If	it rains	I'll	take an umbrella.
	it's sunny	I won't	

c Look at the picture. Write as many sentences as possible with *if* . . .

Example: If the car hits the bicycle, the boy will fall off.

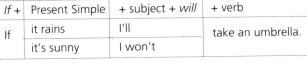

9 Face value

Must be/might be/can't be

An event seen from one point of view . . . gives one impression.

1 Preparation

1 **Work with other students. What do you think is happening in this photograph? Make up a story by answering these questions.**

1 How did the story begin?
2 What has just happened?
3 What is going to happen next?
4 How will it end?

2 **Tell another group of students your story.**

1 What is the main thing your stories have in common?
2 What is the main difference?

3 **Look at the photograph on page 126. What is the real story? What is the point of the photographs?**

2 Grammar: *must be/might be/can't be*

1 **Match sentences with the same meaning from column A and B.**

How sure?	A	B
100% Yes	He is definitely a criminal.	He isn't a criminal.
	I'm sure he's a criminal.	He can't be a criminal.
50%	Perhaps he's a criminal.	He must be a criminal.
	I'm sure he isn't a criminal	He is a criminal.
100% No	He definitely isn't a criminal.	He might be a criminal.

2 🖳 **Listen and repeat the sentences with *must, might* and *can't be*. Can you hear the /t/ sound at the end of these words?**

3 **What do you think? Tell another student why the young man in the photograph above;**

a) must be a kind person.
b) can't be a businessman.
c) might be a rebel.

4 **Make two other sentences which mean 'Perhaps he's a criminal', using *could* and *may*.**

3 Speaking

1 Read the short story below. Why is it strange?

> A man goes into a bar and asks for a glass of water. The barman takes out a gun and points it at the man. The man thanks the barman and leaves the bar.

2 Read the story again. Do you think these sentences are true (T), false (F) or you don't know (DK)?

1 The man is thirsty.
2 The weather is hot.
3 The barman is happy with the man's request.
4 The man is pleased with the barman's reaction.
5 The barman is a criminal.
6 The man is dead by the end of the story.

3 Compare your answers with another student. Justify your answers using *must be/might be/can't be*.

Example: He must be thirsty because he asks for a glass of water.

4 Ask your teacher questions to solve the mystery. She/He can only answer *yes*, *no* or *not important*.

> **NB** *look* vs *look like*
>
> She *looks* friendly.
> She *looks like* an American film star.
>
> **Which is followed by an adjective on its own, *looks* or *looks like*?**

4 Vocabulary: describing people

1 Look at the pairs of adjectives below. Which word describes someone who:

a) doesn't like spending money on her/himself or other people?
b) likes spending time with other people?
c) doesn't mind waiting?
d) thinks their own appearance is very important?
e) is quiet and kind?
f) doesn't frighten anyone?
g) is uncomfortable with new people?
h) shows their love with candles, chocolate, flowers, etc?

Adjectives

gentle/aggressive	mean/generous
patient/impatient	threatening/unthreatening
romantic/unromantic	vain/modest
sociable/unsociable	confident/shy

2 Look at the photographs below with another student. What do you think?

1 How old could each person be?
2 What sort of job might she/he have?
3 Who looks the most aggressive/gentle/vain?
4 Which three adjectives from the list above best describe each person?

5 Reading

1 Read how a panel of six judges saw the faces on page 55. Which person do they think is:

a) the most aggressive?
b) the most gentle?
c) the most vain?

2 Read the texts again and answer these questions.

1 Which of the adjectives you chose for each person appear in the text?
2 Do any of the adjectives chosen by the panellists surprise you?

3 Now turn to page 124 and read what the people themselves think. Answer these questions for each person.

1 Do they generally think the panel was correct?
2 Where do they disagree with the panel's description?

6 Writing

1 Complete the chart with *really/very/quite*.

+	++	+++	++++
. . . shy	shy	. . . shy	. . . shy

2 Write a description of *your* character, using *really/very/quite* + adjectives.

3 Guess who people are from descriptions your teacher reads.

7 Speaking

1 Put these things in order of importance. How do you judge people when you first meet them?

a) type/colour of clothes   c) shoes   e) hair
b) physical appearance   d) face   f) other

2 Tell another student about a particular friend. How did you meet? What things attracted you?

From *New Woman*

FACE VALUES

How much do other people judge you from your face? We showed six people's photographs to a panel and asked for their comments. Then the victims were given a chance to reply...

The panel thought:

1 The panel react immediately to Tina's very short hair, interpreting it as a statement of aggression: 'She looks as hard as nails'. Her mouth is described as threatening. 'She has a mean, unfriendly top lip.' She is also seen as secretive and generally unsociable. But one panellist sees her as gentle and generous with her money. One of the panel want to meet Tina.

2 The panel generally consider Mark to be threatening. Eyebrows that nearly meet in the middle suggest aggression. Mark probably works in an artistic field – 'the theatre or gymnastics' – and is very impatient and unromantic. He is described as sociable and friendly (but this can change!) and vain. He's a dancer or keep-fit fanatic, who brushes his eyebrows in front of the mirror. Two of the panel want to meet him.

3 The panel warm immediately to Elizabeth. They used all the gentle, patient and honest adjectives without hesitation. If she were a dog, people would pat her on the head. Her hair style, off her face, suggests she does organised work; she could be a nurse or a dental receptionist. Surprisingly, all the panel see her as threatening, especially the men! But she could be romantic. Four of the panel want to meet her.

8 Listening

1 **Before you listen to the singer, Phil Collins, put these words in the correct place and form in the text below.**

an audience   a stage   a band   a tape   to applaud
to play   to sing   a song   a concert

Monday 15th

Yesterday night I went to this fantastic Phil
Collins ¹_____ at the Royal Albert Hall. He ²_____ all
his best ³_____ and at the end the ⁴_____ all stood
up and ⁵_____ for ages. Finally, he came back on
⁶_____ and everyone was quiet. Then he ⁷_____ this
incredible drum solo for about fifteen minutes, and then
each member of the ⁸_____ had a chance to play a solo.
It was brilliant. After it finished, I went out and
bought the ⁹_____ and I've been playing it ever since.

2  **Listen to a song written by Phil Collins. What is the song about? Write down the words of the chorus.**

3 **Look at the words of the song on page 132.**

1 Why does time pass slowly for the singer? (Verse 1)
2 Is he happy? Why/Why not? (Verse 2)
3 How does the other person feel about him? (Verse 3)
4 Is it easy for him to say what he feels? (Verse 4)

4 **Listen to an interview with Phil Collins.**

1 What question do you think the interviewer has just asked him?
2 List the countries he mentions.

5 **Listen again and list the countries in the correct column below.**

Countries he has *already* visited	Countries he hasn't visited *yet*

6 **Check your answers with another student.**

Example: STUDENT A: Has he been to Japan yet?
            STUDENT B: No, not yet./Yes, he's already been there.

Speaking

Phil Collins says, 'different nationalities have all got their own little identity.' Talk to other students about your own nationality. What do you think?

1 How do other nationalities see you? Are you *polite/romantic/hard-working/friendly/open/generous . . .?*
2 Is it fair? How do *you* see a typical person from your country?

ENGLISH IN ACTION

You're going to find out about each other's favourite songs.

1 Choose a British/American song that you like.

2 Write the words of the song. Find out the meaning of any difficult words/expressions by using a dictionary or asking an English speaker.

3 Prepare to tell the rest of your class a little about the person/group who sings it. Make notes about who they are, where they come from, the kind of songs they sing, etc.

Prepare to play your song to the class.

4 Tell the class about the singer/s.

5 Give them the words to look at. Explain any difficult words/expressions.

6 Play your song to the class.

7 Vote on the song you liked best.

You are going to a record shop to buy a new album.

8 ▣ Listen to this conversation in a record shop.
   1 What song does the customer want?
   2 Who is it by?
   3 What album is it on?
   4 Does she want a tape, a CD or a record?

9 Listen again and practise a similar conversation with another student. Ask about the song you heard and liked best today.

Language review 9

1 Must be/might be/can't be

These words express degrees of certainty. They say how sure you are.

100% Yes	It is	
↑	It *must be*	
50%	It *might be*	the postman.
↓	It *can't be*	
100% No	It isn't	

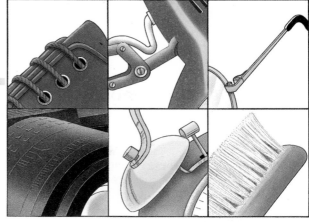

a Look at these objects. Say what you think they are.
Example: It might be a . . . .

b Rephrase the underlined parts of these sentences using *must be*, *might be* or *can't be*, keeping the same meaning.

1 Perhaps Isabel is late for the cinema because she had to work late tonight.
2 I'm sure it isn't 6 o'clock. It was 5.30 only ten minutes ago.
3 They are definitely Maria's brothers. They look just like her.
4 He is really stupid if he thinks I believe him.
5 He definitely isn't your friend. He never says a kind word about you.
6 Maybe she is tired because she got up so early this morning.

2 Look vs look like

- **Look + adjective is used to describe people, places or things and say how they seem.**
She *looks tired*.
The city *looks beautiful* in the sun.

- **Look like + noun (with or without an adjective) is used to make comparisons.**
She *looks like* an Italian *actress*.

c Complete these sentences with the correct form of *look* or *look like*.

1 I think that's her brother. He really . . . her.
2 Why don't you sit down? You . . . tired.
3 Paris . . . really beautiful in the spring.
4 I don't like those trousers. They make me . . . an elephant!
5 He must be in the army. He certainly . . . a soldier.
6 What's wrong? Why do you . . . so unhappy.
7 Who do you . . ., your mother or your father?
8 I don't want to go out. It . . . really cold.
9 They . . . charming but I hear they are very unkind.
10 Your new dress . . . wonderful!

3 Present Perfect + *yet* and *already*

The indefinite time expressions *yet* and *already* can be used with the Present Perfect to mean 'at any time up to now'.

Positive
They've *already* arrived.

Negative
They haven't arrived *yet*.

Question
Have they arrived *yet*?

Short answers
Yes, they have./No, they haven't./No, not *yet*.

d Complete these two dialogues with *yet* or *already*.

1 A: Have you seen Cher's new film . . .?
   B: No, not . . . Have you?
   A: No. But Françoise has . . . seen it and says it's wonderful.

2 C: I have . . . told you, you can't have a new bike . . . We haven't got enough money.
   D: I know but I'm trying to save the money myself. I've . . . got more than half the money I need.
   C: How much have you got?
   D: Not enough . . . But I've told the man in the shop I'll buy it before Christmas!

10 Consolidation

1 Across cultures: money

> **Revises**
> **Vocabulary**: Goods and presents
> **Grammar**: Present Simple (habits); *usually/often/ never*, Present Perfect + *just*; Present Continuous; comparatives and superlatives

1 **Work with other students. Discuss people's attitude to money. What do people in your country usually do in these situations?**

1 They go to a restaurant and the service is poor. Do they leave a tip?
2 They can't think what to give their ten-year-old daughter for her birthday. Do they give her money?
3 They ask friends to go to a restaurant with them. Do they ask them to pay half the bill?
4 They meet someone with a lot more money than they have. Do they let the other person pay for an evening out?
5 They find a small amount of money in the street. Do they take it to the police station?
6 Their school-age child needs more money. Do they suggest she/he earns it by doing housework or a Saturday job?
7 Their friend borrows the money for a packet of cigarettes, then tries to pay them back. Do they accept the money?
8 They are stopped by a policeman for driving too fast. Do they offer him money?
9 A man takes a woman out for the evening. Does he pay for both of them?

2 📼 **Listen to an American and a British person discussing some of the situations in the last exercise. Which do they discuss?**

3 **Listen again. What are their answers to the questions discussed? Do any surprise you?**

4 **Read the cartoon below.**

1 What is the relationship between the people?
2 What is the joke? Do you think it's funny?

5 **Retell the joke by answering these questions.**

1 What is each person doing in the first picture?
2 What has the woman just read in the second picture?
3 Why is the man laughing?
4 Why isn't he laughing in the third picture?

From *The Daily Express*

6 Point at these things in the photograph above.

a book   a plane ticket
a packet of coffee   a packet of cigarettes
a banana   a packet of tea
a lamp   a compact disc
flowers   a bottle of perfume
a jacket   a box of chocolates
a bottle of wine

7 Put the things listed above in order by price. Which is the most expensive and which is the cheapest in your country?

8 Compare your answers with another student. What are the differences, if any?

9 Talk to your partner about the things above.

1 Which have you often received as presents?
2 Which have you never received as presents?
3 When might you receive the more unusual presents?

10 Talk to other students about present-giving in your family/country.

1 On which of these occasions do you usually give people presents?

    a) a birthday
    b) a religious festival
    c) a wedding
    d) the birth of a baby
    e) after a holiday
    f) when people change jobs or homes
    g) when you visit people for dinner
    h) any other time

2 What sort of presents do you give on the occasions above? Which of these people do you usually give presents to?
    children   family   anyone else?
    colleagues friends

3 What do you think? Has present-giving become too commercial? Or do you really enjoy giving/receiving presents?

2 Language in context: shopping

Revises
Vocabulary: Shopping
Grammar: *Might be/can't be/must be*; Present Perfect + *just*

1 Work with another student. Look at the people with their shopping in the article below. Guess what they've just bought.

- **Example:** A: It might be a packet of tea.
  - B: No, it can't be. It's too big.

2 Read the texts quickly. Were you right? What has each person just bought?

3 Read the texts again. Discuss these questions.

1 How planned was each person's shopping?
2 What is their attitude to spending money?
3 Who is the most careful/extravagant with money?

4 Ask other students what they have bought in the last week.

1 Are most people in your group careful or extravagant with money?
2 Do they generally plan what they buy?
3 How often do they buy on impulse?
4 What did they last buy on impulse?

HEY BIG SPENDER!

It's Saturday afternoon and everyone is spending money. But what do they buy? Paul Stewart went to Bristol to find out..

Ian Bennett
photographer
'I buy as I need. I've just bought a packet of coffee and some fruit for breakfast, bananas actually. I don't go shopping on any particular day. If I'm hungry, I buy.'

Kate Goodwin
school theatre company worker
'I've just bought a book. I like spending money just because I've got it. I simply love shopping! I've wanted to read this book for ages.'

Bayo Harding
student
'I spend my money on travel. I've just bought a holiday. I had to work in McDonald's for months but it's worth it. I'm off to the sun next week.'

Jeanne Wilton
disc jockey
'I spend most of my money on clothes. I buy something every month. This month it's a skirt. Last month a jacket. I earn it so…I spend it!'

From Company

3 Thinking about learning: approaches

Revises
Vocabulary: *Look/feel/taste/sound/smell + like*; the body
Grammar: *Don't mind + -ing* form; *If + present + will*

1 Talk to other students. Answer these questions about the skills below.

1 Which of these things have you learned successfully? Who taught you?
2 How did you learn? Did you read instructions, watch other people, have lessons or do something else?

to drive a car	to play a musical instrument
to dance	to use a washing machine
to type	to read
to cook	to swim

2 ▣ Listen to these people talking about languages they have learned in different ways.

1 What language did they learn?
2 How did they learn it?
3 Are they generally positive or negative about the experience?

3 Listen again and complete the chart. How do they feel about the activities they mention?

	liked	didn't mind	didn't like
1	*watching videos*		
2			
3			

4 Talk to your partner. What do you feel about the things the three people mentioned?

5 Look at the advertisements on this page.

1 What are they advertising?
2 What do they promise if you buy their course?
3 What will they do if you are not satisfied?
4 Which of your senses do they say help you learn faster?

6 Match the verbs of the senses to the parts of the body.

A	B
look like	ears
feel like	nose
taste like	eyes
sound like	mouth
smell like	hands

From the **BBC**

The Video Language Course for Children

With this course, your children will love learning a new language

Everything needed is included. Four video cassettes; two audio cassettes; an activity book and a video story book.
Through *listen-and-learn* and *see-and-learn*, your child will make rapid progress and begin speaking a foreign language from the very first day! He or she can learn alone, or you can help – and learn the language, too!

No risk guarantee

And there's no risk! If you and your child are not absolutely delighted, you may return the course within 30 days for a full refund.

In French, English, Spanish, Italian or German

You can be confident in FRENCH, SPANISH, GERMAN or ITALIAN in 3 1/2 weeks.

With Accelerated Learning, you learn a new language exactly the same way that you learned your first language. By seeing, hearing and doing. Learning is fast. And fun.

Release your natural ability to learn
Unlike other systems, Accelerated Learning uses <u>all</u> the natural ways and senses to help you absorb a language. It links dramatic presentation, entertaining games and music with your own mental images.
Because you use your whole brain, you learn more quickly and enjoy it. In a matter of weeks, you can be speaking your new language confidently.

15 DAY FREE TRIAL If you are not totally happy with your progress, you can return the course and will have paid nothing.

⚠ accelerated learning

7 Use one of the verbs + *like* in column A to complete these sentences.

1 I can't see what's in this envelope but it . . . a cassette.
2 He's very handsome. He . . . the actor in last night's film.
3 This tea is terrible. It . . . washing-up water.
4 I love this perfume. It . . . roses.
5 What is that noise in the bedroom? It . . . a train.

Check What You Know!
Now turn to page 128 and complete Check What You Know 2.

Images

Find out what kind of learner you are. Is it

easier for you to imagine what things look,

feel, smell, taste or sound like?

1 Read the questions below. Close your eyes
and imagine each thing. How clear is your
image? Open your eyes and write a number
next to each one, like this:

no image   = 0
an unclear image = 1
a clear image   = 2

1 What do these things look like:
   a) birds flying?
   b) pink flowers with green leaves?
   c) your name on an envelope?
2 What do these things feel like:
   a) a cat?
   b) a snowball?
   c) swimming in the sea?
3 What do these things sound like:
   a) a telephone ringing?
   b) a plane in the sky?
   c) a stone falling in a pond?
4 What do these things smell like:
   a) petrol?
   b) fresh coffee?
   c) old fish?
5 What do these things taste like:
   a) toothpaste?
   b) salt?
   c) chocolate?

2 How many points did you get for each group
of questions? Tell another student which
group you found easiest to imagine.

3 First, take a few deep breaths.

4 🖥 Now, listen and look at the picture.

5 Close your eyes as you go through the door
in the picture. Continue to imagine as you
listen to the cassette.

6 Talk to another student. Say what you
remember about the garden on the other
side of the door.

11 *Changes*

Been vs *gone*

1 Preparation

1 Before you listen to a song from the 1960s, answer these questions.

1 What is happening in each photograph above?
2 What do you think the song will be about?

2 📼 Listen to the song. Which of the things or people in the photographs does it mention?

3 Listen again. A new question is asked in each verse.

1 What is the question?
2 What is the answer?

4 What do you think?

1 Is the song about love or war?
2 What question does the singer ask about the future? Is she optimistic or pessimistic?
3 Do you agree with her?

NB *been* vs *gone*

Where have all the flowers *gone*?
Where have you *been*?

1 Which word means to go and return, *been* or *gone*?
2 Which word means to go and still be absent, *been* or *gone*?

---

2 Speaking

1 Complete the *You* column in the chart below. In what year did you last do these things?

	You	Your partner
Move house		
Have a new hairstyle		
Change jobs/schools		
Meet a new friend/partner		
Go on an exciting holiday		
Act completely out of character		

2 Ask another student when they last did these things. Write her/his dates in the other column.

3 Tell the class something interesting you found out about your partner.

Example: She/He last went on holiday a year ago. She/He went to . . .

3 Grammar: Present Perfect

Unfinished past

> She *has lived* in the same house *since* 1991.

1 Look at the sentence above and answer these questions.

1 Does she live in this house now?
2 When did she move there?
3 What hasn't she done since that date?

2 Use the information from your completed chart in Exercise 2 Speaking to write sentences about your partner. Use positive and/or negative forms.

Example: She has had the same job since . . .
She hasn't moved house since . . .

3 Speak to other students. Find out where they live/work and how long they have lived/worked there. What questions will you ask?

4 Vocabulary

1 Match these nouns to their definitions.

1 birth   a) separating from a wife/husband
2 divorce   b) getting sick/ill
3 redundancy   c) having a lot of money/riches
4 illness   d) being born
5 wealth   e) losing a job because there isn't
                       enough work

2 Complete the words below to make the opposites of the nouns above.

de . . .   ma . . .   em . . .   he . . .   po . . .

3 Check your answers with other students. List the adjectives and verbs from these nouns. Use your mini-dictionary on page 138.

Example: birth (*n.*), be born (*v.*)
death (*n.*), dead (*adj.*), die (*v.*)

4 Talk to another student. What things have most changed your life in the last five years? Was it:

- changing jobs/schools/countries?
- inheriting/winning/losing money?
- meeting a new friend/partner?
- having/looking after a baby?
- something else?

67

5 Reading

1 Work in two groups. Each group read about one couple in the magazine article below and answer these questions.

1 What main thing has happened to change the lives of this couple?
2 Did they feel excited or worried when it happened?
3 How do they feel about it now?

2 Read your part of the article again and write short answers to these questions.

1 When did the main change happen?
2 What other changes have happened? Think about the couple's lifestyle and relationship since the main change.

3 Check your answers with other students in your group.

4 Talk to a student from the other group. Tell your partner about the couple in your article. What has happened to her/his couple?

5 Work with another pair of students. What do you think?

1 Which couple has the biggest problems?
2 What will happen if things continue as they are?
3 What should/shouldn't they do to make life easier?

ALL change

How much pressure could your relationship take?
Two couples describe events that have changed their lives.

Bill (40) and Jane (35) got married last year after living together for ten years. Jane gave up her job as a translator when she discovered she was pregnant. A week after the birth of their daughter, Claudia, Bill was made redundant from the publishing firm he worked for. They live in West London.

Jane: Last year was the best and worst year of my life. Everything happened - Claudia was born, Bill lost his job, I gave up work, my father died and we moved house. In one way Claudia's birth made it all more difficult because I was so tired, but it helped too. When my father died it made me see life as a continuing cycle of birth and death. When Bill was made redundant, we were very worried about the cost of having a child. We soon had to forget our worries and look after her. At first I thought it was good because he could spend time with Claudia. I was sure he would get a job quickly but this was nine months ago and he is still not working and now we are borrowing money. If he doesn't get a job by the end of the year, I will have to go back to work. Bill will have to look after Claudia while I go out to work.

Bill: I never thought I could be made redundant. It was a terrible shock. I didn't realise how quickly I'd start to lose my confidence and self-respect. It feels strange being at home all day, and if I take Claudia out to the park I feel uncomfortable in a world of women. At first I was very depressed. I was very angry with my old employers. Now I'm slowly adapting to my new role and even beginning to enjoy the free time. Money is a big worry though and I just don't know what will happen in the future.

Debbie (26) and Martin (27) have been together for two years and share a house in Fulham, London. Last year, Debbie was offered a job with much more responsibility and a much bigger salary. Martin, an architect, has had to accept a more solitary life.

Debbie: Eighteen months ago, I was offered a very good job with a top management consultancy firm. The salary is three times more than I used to earn. By the end of the first month, I was staying at the office until 8.30 every evening and taking work home with me every weekend. During my second month I got my travelling schedule and I knew that I had to be away from home for at least ten

days every month. Martin was as excited as I was at first, but it wasn't long before it got difficult for him. I was spending a lot of time at breakfast and evening meetings. Superficially I can see that it has changed me. I've bought a complete set of new clothes, I go to the hairdresser's regularly and I have to mix socially with people I don't always like. Martin really hates this. At first I asked him to come with me when I got an invitation for two, now I don't. We live more separate lives than before and that worries me.

Martin: I'm really pleased about Debbie's success but I'm not sure if it's a good idea in the long term. It's OK for the moment but in fact, she is sacrificing herself, her family and her friends for her job. I don't actually like this new situation, I just tolerate it. I used to enjoy our time together and our rather relaxed lifestyle. I don't really like the way things have changed. However I do try to understand because the job's important to Debbie and she's important to me.

6 Grammar: *for/since*

> They have had problems *since* 1990.
> They have had problems *for* . . . years.

1 Look at the sentences above and answer these questions.

1 How many years ago was 1990? Complete the second sentence so it means the same as the first.
2 Which word refers to an exact point in time, *for* or *since*?
3 Which word refers to a period of time, *for* or *since*?

2 Look at this time-line. Put *for* and *since* in the correct place.

3 Put these time words/expressions in the correct column below.

many years	we last met	a long time
1990	last night	the summer
April 29th	two weeks	ages
three days	3.30	a while
yesterday	a few months	January
ten minutes	1987	Monday

For	Since
many years	*1990*

Pronunciation

1 🖵 Listen and repeat the expressions in the *for* column above.

2 Listen again. When you hear /r/ at the end of *for*, mark the expressions, like this:

/ə/
for a few months

3 Work with another student. Say each expression in the *for* column and make one or two other similar expressions.

Example: For many years. For a few years. For three years.

7 Speaking

1 Look at the list of possessions below. Which of them have you or your family got? Which haven't you got? Tell other students how long you have had these things.

a car   a walkman   a bicycle
a pet   a camera   a computer

2 Tell another student about the last time you got a present.

1 What did you get?
2 What was the occasion?
3 Who gave it to you?

Grammar: *give* + two objects

> a) His mother gave him a watch.
> b) His mother gave it to him.

1 Look at the sentences above with another student. Answer these questions.

1 What did his mother give?
2 Who did she give it to?
3 Which comes first in sentence a), *the thing* she gave or *the person* she gave it to?
4 Which comes first in sentence b), *the thing* she gave or *the person* she gave it to?
5 Which preposition goes between *the thing* and *the person* in sentence b)?

2 Rearrange these words to make correct sentences.

1 give tomorrow it me to
2 brother chocolate her gave me some
3 socks every she them Christmas gives
4 perfume has mother he given expensive his

3 Tell another student about your most treasured possession.

1 What is it?
2 Was it a present? If so, who gave it to you?
3 Why did this person give it to you?
4 How long have you had it?
5 Why is it so special?

4 🖵 Listen to three people answering the questions above. Note their answers.

5 Use your notes to talk about their possessions.

ENGLISH IN ACTION

You are going to make a major change.

You'd like to emigrate to Australia.

You will all need character references when

you go to live abroad.

1 Work in two groups. Half of you are Australian Immigration Officials. Half of you are applicants for immigration.

AUSTRALIAN IMMIGRATION OFFICIALS: Follow the instructions on page 125.

APPLICANTS: Follow the instructions below.

1 Prepare to answer an Australian Immigration Official's questions. Look at the photographs of Australia and think about these questions.

   a) What things attract you to Australia? Why do you want to emigrate?

   b) Would you like to live in a big town/the country/by the sea?

   c) What can you/your family offer your new country?

   d) Which two people can you ask to give you references?

2 Have the interview at the Australian Embassy. You need to:

   a) answer the official's questions.

   b) explain why you think you/your family would be good immigrants.

   c) find out what to do next.

2 Another student asks you to write her/his character reference. Look at the model below. What do you need to include?

3 Ask your partner a few questions to get information before you write.

4 Write the reference.

5 Read the reference your partner has written for you. What do you think? Is it fair?

To whom it may concern

I have known Peter Jackson since 1987. We were students together at Durham University and then worked together for a year in Paris. He was a supportive colleague and a good friend. The work we did involved a lot of money and Peter was known for his honesty.

He speaks excellent French. Since working in Paris, he has continued to study languages. He takes classes in Italian and Greek. He has travelled to many countries and is sensitive to different cultures.

He is a hard-working person but he also enjoys his free-time. His many hobbies include tennis, swimming and photography.

Peter has many qualities. He is adventurous but reliable. He has been an excellent friend. I couldn't recommend him more highly.

Language review 11

11

1 Past participles: *been* and *gone*

The verb *go* has two possible participles: *been* and *gone*.

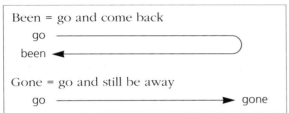

a Complete these sentences with *been* or *gone*.

1 A: Christophe has . . . to India.
   B: I know. When is he coming back?
2 A: How often have you . . . to Canada?
   B: Only once.
3 A: Where have you . . . ?
   B: Just down the road, to post a letter.
4 A: Where is Ravi?
   B: He's not here. I think he's . . . to the shops.

2 Present Perfect: unfinished past

The Present Perfect can be used to talk about situations which started in the past but continue in the present.

Present Simple	Present Perfect
She is in America.	She's been there since June. (**not** *She is there since June.*)
I am married.	How long have you been married? (**not** *How long are you married?*)
I live in London.	I have lived here all my life. (**not** *I live here all my life.*)

b Put the verbs in brackets in the Present Simple or the Present Perfect.

Example: I . . . (live) here since 1989. – I have lived here since 1989.

1 She . . . (live) half the year in France and half the year in Britain.
2 He . . . (work) for them on Tuesdays and Fridays.
3 How many times . . . he (work) for them?
4 How long . . . you (know) Maria?
5 I . . . (not know) Maria.
6 We . . . (have) a new car.
7 We . . . (have) it since Tuesday.

3 *For/since*

We use *for* and *since* to say *how long*. *For* refers to a period of time. *Since* refers to a point in time.

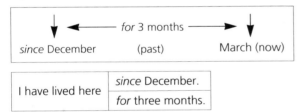

I have lived here	*since* December.
	for three months.

c Use *for* or *since* to join these sentences.

Example: I am in the office. I arrived two hours ago – I have been in the office for two hours.

1 We know Carlos. We first met him in 1990.
2 They are married. They got married a long time ago.
3 He lives in San Francisco. He moved there 18 months ago.
4 She is in hospital. She went in on Saturday.
5 She's a teacher. She trained 3 years ago.

4 *Give* + two objects

Example 1

Give	+ a person	+ a thing
I gave	my friend	the money.

Example 2

Give	+ a thing	+ *to*	+ a person
I gave	the money	to	my friend.
	it		her.

We generally use example 1 when we use two nouns. We generally use example 2 when we use the pronoun *it* or *them*.

d Write sentences to say who gave these things to these people for their birthdays.

Example: Paolo got a watch from Luc. – He gave Paolo a watch.

1 Christopher got a pen and a book from Sally.
2 Sophie got a camera from Tony.
3 Ali got a shirt and tie. They were from José.

e Now answer these questions.

Example: Who did Luc give the watch to? He gave it to Paolo.

1 Who did Sally give the pen and book to?
2 Who did Tony give the camera to?
3 Who did José give the shirt and tie to?

2 Speaking

1 What do you think? Which of these things can you usually remember for a long time? Which do you forget?

a) names of people
b) a good/bad childhood experience
c) poems learned by heart
d) lunch on a typical day a week ago
e) names of everyday objects
f) information learned for exams
g) dates things happened in your life
h) telephone numbers
i) your reaction to an important historical event
j) an embarrassing situation
k) faces you've seen before

2 Tell another student what you think. Do you agree?

3 Look at the article below. Find out what the scientists think.

1 Which things do we remember most easily?
2 Which do we forget?
3 Do you agree with their opinion? Why/Why not?

MEMORY

Our memory can hold a lot of information but it is not limitless; we forget small details and so have more room for important memories. We do not usually forget our most pleasant experiences, things that interest us and things we have a special reason to remember. For example, ten years after the assassination of US President John F. Kennedy, many people remembered exactly how they first heard the news of the president's death.

We also remember particularly well the things we think about immediately before we go to sleep.

The things we most often forget are names (of things as well as people), numbers, dates, information learned especially for exams, and things we do not understand or find interesting. We also find it hard to remember things when we are embarrassed, ill or very tired. In fact, we forget routine, everyday things all the time, and it is perfectly normal.

We could make our memory better but unfortunately we have very little control over what we forget. We might want to forget something we do not like but our memory won't do it.

From Best

1 Preparation

1 Test your memory. Look at the objects above for two minutes, then shut your book. Write what you remember.

2 Check your answers with another student, like this:

/wəz/   /wə/
Example: There was a pen. There were two apples.

3 Listening

1 Before you listen, do you remember when these things happened? Make sentences, using the table below.

• Elvis Presley died		April 1992.
• There was a big earthquake in San Francisco		February 1990.
• The Berlin wall came down	in	August 1977.
• Marlene Dietrich died		April 1906.
• Nelson Mandela was released		November 1989.

2 ▣ Listen to people remembering some of these events. Write the number of the conversation next to the event they remember.

Example: Marlene Dietrich died. (1).

3 Listen again. Which of these things was each person doing when they heard the news? Write the number of the conversation next to the activity.

a) listening to the radio
b) buying an ice-cream
c) watching TV
d) talking on the phone
e) shaving
f) watching an opera
g) playing tennis

4 Grammar: Past Continuous

Interrupted action

1st clause		2nd clause
I was shaving	when	she told me the news.
She told me the news		I was shaving.

Look at the sentences above. Answer these questions with another student.

1 Which two actions are referred to in both sentences?
2 Which action started first? Which action interrupted it?
3 Which verb is in the Past Simple? Which verb is in the Past Continuous?
4 How do you form the Past Continuous, its negative and question form?

Pronunciation

1 ▣ Listen to the sentences in the box above. Which word is stressed in each clause? How do you say *was*?

2 Listen and repeat the sentences.

1 Does your voice go up or down at the end of the 1st clause? Is the sentence finished?
2 Does your voice go up or down at the end of the 2nd clause? Is the sentence finished?

3 Practise saying similar sentences. Use your answers to Exercise 3 Listening.

Example: The first person was buying an ice-cream when she heard about Marlene Dietrich.

4 Play a memory game.

1 Choose one of these actions, or something else, to mime.

- eating spaghetti
- shaving
- climbing a ladder
- playing the piano
- playing golf
- painting a picture

2 Mime the action until your teacher says 'Stop'. Remember what other students are doing.
3 Work with another student and write what you remember. What were other students doing? How many actions can you remember between you?

Example: Roberto was shaving when she said 'Stop'.

Jane Rule
MEMORY BOARD

From *Memory Board* by Jane Rule
(Pandora Press 1987)

MEMORY BOARD   65

'Have I had my shower?'
'No,' Diana said, smiling.
While Constance showered, Diana took up a small slate, lifted the cellophane to clear it of the crossed-off items of yesterday, and began to write the list for today, the first item intended to amuse Constance.

Put on your clothes
Breakfast
The morning show ¹
Lift bulbs in the bed ² *by the garage*
Lunch
Rest
*Errands,*³ *on the avenue*
Walk on the beach
Dinner with David

Constance arrived at the breakfast table, dressed, with the slate in her hand, the first item crossed off.
'David who?' she asked.
'My brother.'
Constance stared away at the blank slate or her memory.
'My twin brother.'
'Is it your birthday?' Constance asked in sudden agitation.
'No, no of course not.'
'Then why is he coming'
'I'm not really sure. He invited himself.'
'With ...' Constance paused.
'His wife died last year,' Diana reminded her.
There were times when Diana envied Constance's memory loss.

> Glossary ¹ show = television programme ² bed = flower bed
> ³ errands = shopping

5   Reading

1 Before you read an extract from the novel *Memory Board,* look at the photograph of the slate above.

1 What is a slate used for?
2 Why are the first two items crossed off?
3 How does the cellophane clear the slate?

2 Read the extract from *Memory Board* and answer these questions.

1 Why is a slate important in this story?
2 Who are the three people? What is the relationship between them?

3 Read the extract again and answer these questions.

1 Why does Constance need to ask the first question?
2 How often does Diana write on the slate?
3 What did Diana write to amuse Constance? Why would it amuse her?
4 What does David usually do on Diana's birthday?
5 Why does Diana think Constance is lucky?

4 Look at the words on Constance's memory board and number these actions in the order she did them.

a) relax
b) have something to eat
c) have something to eat
d) have something to eat
e) watch TV
f) do some gardening
g) go for a walk
h) get dressed (1)
i) go shopping

> **NB**   *remember vs remind*
>
> Constance can't *remember* David.
> Diana *reminds* her who he is.
>
> 1 Which means to have a memory, *remember* or *remind?*
> 2 Which means to help someone remember, *remember* or *remind?*

6 Writing

1 These words go at the beginning or end of sentences to link ideas in the same paragraph.

next   then   finally   after that   first

1 Which one can begin a paragraph?
2 Which one can begin the last sentence?
3 Which three go in the middle, in any order?

2 **Write a paragraph. Say what Constance did, based on the day from her memory board.**

3 **Write your own memory board for tomorrow.**

4 **Read your partner's memory board and tell the class what she/he's going to do.**

Example: First, Danuta is going to get up early.

> **NB** *some vs any*
>
> Do you need *any* meat or fish?
> I need *some* meat, but I don't need *any* fish.
>
> *Some* is generally used in positive sentences. When is *any* generally used?

7 Vocabulary: shops and products

1 📺 **Listen and repeat these words. Is the final 's' pronounced /s/, /z/ or /ɪz/?**

ice creams   aspirins   crisps
sandwiches   lamb chops   stamps
traveller's cheques

2 **Match one of these things to each place in the photographs below. Make sentences like this:**

You can get ice creams at the newsagent's.

3 **With another student, write down two more things you can get in each place.**

4 **Now, make your own shopping list of things you need to buy. Write one thing for each place.**

Grammar: infinitive of purpose

Ask your partner questions about their shopping list. Use the names of the places below, like this:

Example: A: Why are you going to the butcher's?
         B: (Because I want) *To get* some meat.

One way to remember a list of things you have to do is to imagine the shops in your street and to walk down it putting items along the route. The stranger it looks, the easier it will be to remember. This is called the LOCI method.

From *The Sunday Times Magazine*

Learn the LOCI method to help you remember better.

1 Read the extract from The *Sunday Times Magazine*. What is the LOCI method?

2 Check your answer with another student. Then look at the picture, drawn before the artist went skiing. What do you think? What did the artist want to remember?

3 Turn to page 125 and check your answers. Did you guess correctly?

4 **Draw your own LOCI map.**

1 Use your 'memory board' list from Exercise 6 Writing on page 75. What do you need to remember to do tomorrow?

2 Draw a map of your favourite shopping street. Put the things to remember on it.

3 Give it to another student.

5 Look at your partner's map. Tell her/him what you think she/he has to remember. Ask questions if you don't understand.

Example: A: Why have you drawn a flower?
B: To remind me to buy flowers for my mother.

Language review 12

12

1 Verbs

• **Past Continuous (interrupted action)**

We can use the Past Continuous to talk about an action which was in progress when another action interrupted it.

He *was read*ing when the phone rang.
The phone rang when he *was read*ing.

He began reading (past)   The phone rang

He was reading

• **Infinitive of purpose**

To say why a person does something, use *to* + verb.

A: Why did you go to the shops?
B: *To get* some food.

a Make sentences from the words below. Put one verb in the Past Simple and one verb in the Past Continuous.

Example: phone/ring/I/have bath. – I was having a bath when the phone rang.

1 it/start/rain/I/drive/work.
2 they/have/breakfast/post/arrive.
3 he/dream/girlfriend/alarm clock/go/off.
4 he/make/dinner/she/tell/him/news.

b Write as many reasons as possible in answer to these questions. Use *to* + verb.

Example: Why do you go to a pub? – *To* get a drink./ *To* meet friends.

Why do you go to:	Why do you buy:
1 a bank?	1 a newspaper?
2 a library?	2 a bicycle?
3 an art gallery?	3 a hammer and nails?
	4 a needle and cotton?

2 Some/any

Some is generally used in positive sentences. *Any* is generally used in negative sentences and questions.

	Positive	Negative	Question
Uncountable	some	not any	any
Countable plural	some	not any	any

I've got *some* tea but I haven't got *any* coffee.
Have you got *any*?
I've got *some* cakes but I haven't got *any* biscuits.
Have you got *any*?

c Complete this conversation with *some* or *any*.

A: Have you got (1) . . . records by Sting?
B: Yes, look over there. There are (2) . . . on that chair.
A: Great! I haven't heard (3) . . . Sting songs for ages. My brother's got (4) . . . old Police records but he hasn't got (5) . . . by Sting, on his own. I'm sorry, I can't see (6) . . . here. There are (7) . . . Simply Red and U2 records but nothing by Sting.
B: Oh, wait a minute. I've lent (8) . . . of my records to Pam. She's probably got them. Put something else on. Can you see (9) . . . other records you like?

3 Sequencers

Sequencers link ideas and can begin or end a sentence.

First,	A	
Then,
Next,
After that,	B/C/D	happened.
Finally,	E	

d Write about Alfonso's day yesterday. Use one or two sequencers, and begin like this:

Yesterday Alfonso had a disastrous day. First . . .

Subject and object questions;
political leaders

1 Preparation

1 Match the quotes to the famous people in the photographs below.

2 Look at the quotes and photographs. Who was speaking:

a) at a political rally? e) on the radio?
b) to his mistress? f) to members of the
c) to himself? government?
d) about the poor?

3 Write complete sentences. What was each person doing when she/he said the famous words?

Example: Napoleon was speaking to his mistress when he said 'Not tonight, Josephine!'

2 Grammar: subject questions

Subject	Object

Napoleon spoke to Josephine.

a) Who spoke to Josephine?

b) Who did he speak to?

1 Look at the subject and object questions above.

1 What is the answer to each question, a) and b)?
2 In which question is the auxiliary verb used, a) or b)?
3 In which question does *who* come directly before the main verb?

2 Complete these questions to find out more about Napoleon.

Example: Napoleon was Emperor of France. – When was he Emperor of France?

1 People adored him. Who . . .?
2 He won a lot of battles. Which battles . . .?
3 Something went wrong. What . . .?
4 An English Admiral captured Napoleon. Who . . .?
5 He lived in exile. Where . . .?
6 He died. How . . . ? When . . .?

3 Speak to other students. How many questions can you answer?

Vocabulary: political leaders

1 Use these words to describe the famous people on this page.

an empress/emperor a prime minister a president
a prince/princess a queen/king a politician

2 🔲 Listen. Check your answers and mark the stress on the words.

3 Name other people with these roles. Where are/were they from?

To be or not to be, that is the question.

I have a dream.

Let them eat cake! We shall fight on the beaches.

There will be no whitewash at the White House.

Not tonight, Josephine.

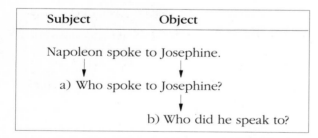

Winston Churchill

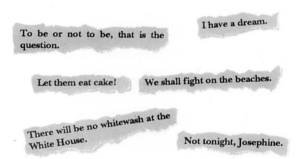

Napoleon Bonaparte

Martin Luther King

Hamlet

Richard Nixon

Marie-Antoinette

Politics

Political Systems

In Britain there is an <u>election</u> at least every four years when people <u>vote</u> for different political parties. In Britain there are three main parties. The Conservative Party is traditionally a right-wing party. The Labour party is a left-wing party and the Liberal Democratic Party is a centre party. The <u>party</u> with the most elected <u>Members of Parliament</u> (MPs) becomes the government and is responsible for making the <u>laws</u> of the country. The <u>leader</u> of the government is called the Prime Minister. The party with the second largest number of MPs forms the <u>opposition</u>.

In the United States, there are Presidential Elections every four years. At this time people vote directly for the person they want to become President. It is possible to become President and not to be the leader of the party in government. There are two main parties, the Republicans and the Democrats; both have politicians with many different views.

In Australia, there are four main political parties and the head of the government is the Prime Minister. People have to vote in general elections or they break the law.

Australia and other countries, as different as New Zealand, India and Jamaica, are politically independent of Britain but are linked by the British royal family. They have the same king or queen as the British people.

3 Reading

1 Read the text about government in different English-speaking countries. Answer these questions.

1 Which three countries is the text mainly about?
2 How many main political parties do they have?
3 Which have a president?
4 Which have a prime minister?
5 Which other English-speaking countries are mentioned?
6 Which countries in the text have a queen/king?

2 Look at the underlined words in the first paragraph of the text above. Find the word that means:

1 the head of a political group. (*n.*)
2 a time when we choose politicians for government. (*n.*)
3 the second largest group of elected politicians. (*n.*)
4 to choose a person (usually secretly) for government. (*v.*)
5 an organisation of people with the same political ideas. (*n.*)
6 elected members of the British government. (*n.*)
7 rules made by the government. (*n.*)

Pronunciation: word families

1 Work with another student. Look at the words below and answer these questions.

1 Are they nouns, adjectives or verbs?
2 Which of the nouns refer to a person?

Example: politics (*n.*) politician (*n.* = a person) political (*adj.*)

1 leader, lead
2 election, elect, elected
3 opposition, oppose
4 vote, voter
5 law, lawyer
6 government, govern

2 🖳 Listen and mark the stress on the words.

3 Listen again. Find the words with the sounds:

/ɒ/   /ɔː/   /əʊ/
cot   caught   coat

4 Speak to other students about the political system in your country. Answer these questions.

1 Is it like any of the systems in the text above? If not, how is it different?
2 What sort of leader do you have?
3 How often do you have elections?
4 When can you vote? Do you have to vote?
5 How many political parties are there?

4   Vocabulary: political issues

1   Work with other students. Which of the political issues below is concerned with:

1   the physical condition of the world?
2   medicine and hospitals?
3   the need for work?
4   the army?
5   the organisation of money, trade and industry?
6   looking after children?
7   the money the government takes from salaries?
8   schools and learning?
9   money for old people?

a) unemployment   d) childcare   g) health
b) education   e) defence   h) pensions
c) the environment f) the economy i) taxation

2   What do you think? Put the political issues in order of importance for today's world.

5   Reading

Look at the election leaflets below. Answer these questions.

1   Which British political party is each one for?
2   Which issues above are mentioned by:

a)   all three parties?
b)   two parties?
c)   only one party?

Grammar: *will* (promises)

| We'll cut taxation | *as soon as* we are elected. |
| We won't increase taxation | |

1   Look at the example above and answer these questions.

1   What time is referred to, present or future?
2   What word could replace the time expression *as soon as*?
3   Is the verb after the time expression in a present or future form?

2   Work in groups of three. Each student look at a different election leaflet below. Say what your party promises to do as soon as they get elected.

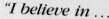

Liberty   Prosperity   Justice

1 Labour and the economy
- Introduce a fair minimum wage
- Invest in high technology and research
- Invest in public transport
- Address the problems of unemployment
- Real jobs and training for young people

2 Labour for the young and old
- Big increase in Child Benefit to go to mothers
- Increase the pension by £5 a week for the single person and £8 for a married couple

3 Labour for health
- Modernise not privatise the Health Service
- Address the real causes of ill-health, such as poverty and poor housing

4 Labour for education
- Nursery education for all
- Money to repair school buildings

Labour

Liberal Democrat

MY VOTE for a prosperous and enterprising economy
Long term economic success depends on the highest quality education and training, investing in industry with real potential, and working with our European partners.

MY VOTE for education and a skilled society
Committed professional teachers will be recognised and rewarded; every child will be entitled to nursery schooling. Education and training at every level will be improved.
All parties claim to care about education. Only the Liberal Democrats are prepared to add a penny on income tax to ensure that our children are properly educated.

MY VOTE for a cleaner and greener environment
Britain is fast becoming Western Europe's dirtiest country. We will make the polluter pay, but create incentives for industries that are clean and don't waste precious resources.

MY VOTE for the NHS and a caring community
The Liberal Democrats are committed to a decent level of health service funding. We will also increase basic pensions. We will take action to combat crime. We want more police to be seen in the streets and based at local police stations.

Vote Conservative X

"I believe in …

1   A strong economy with low inflation. With lower interest rates, we will maintain a healthy economic environment.

2   A free National Health Service offering the best possible treatment to all. Waiting lists should be reduced further.

3   A European Community of Independent States working together, expanding to include the new democracies of eastern Europe.

4   Strong defence for Britain. Our armed forces will have the best and most modern equipment."

6 Listening

1 📻 **Listen to Tony Blair, the British Member of Parliament for the constituency of Sedgefield.**

1 What party is he in?
2 How long has he been in Parliament?
3 What issues does he think are most important
   a) now, and b) in the future?

2 📻 **Listen and complete his diary for next week. Put in these appointments and their times.**

- Chamber of Commerce lunch
- prison reform meeting
- Sunday trading meeting
- conference on crime
- factory open day
- TV recording
- student dinner

Monday –
   4 pm – respond to government's
             immigration proposals
   7 pm – tour of Houses of Parliament

Tuesday – open airport road
   8.30 pm – present education and
             training awards

Wednesday
   am } – constituents' surgeries

Thursday – fire brigade
            meeting

Friday

7 Grammar

Present Continuous (future)

> a) He is talking to a journalist (at the moment).
> b) He is speaking at a conference on Monday.

Look at the sentences in the Present Continuous above, and answer these questions.

1 Which sentence refers to present time, a) or b)?
2 Which sentence refers to future time, a) or b)?
3 What extra information tells you it's future time?

8 Speaking

1 Say each of the times below in two ways.

　　　　　　/θ/　/θ//t/　/f/　/θ/
Example: 3.30 = three thirty/half-past three
   3.00　　3.15　　3.25　　3.35　　3.45　　3.50

2 Say the days of the week. Which days begin with /θ/, /t/, and /f/?

3 Look at Tony Blair's diary with another student. Take it in turns to check what he is doing next week.

Example: A: What is he doing on Monday at ten
                o'clock?
             B: He's speaking at a conference on
                crime.

4 Find a time to have a meal with another student next week. You'll need at least two hours.

STUDENT A: Look at your diary on this page.
STUDENT B: Look at your diary on page 125.

Example:
A: Are you free at half past seven on Friday?
B: I'm really sorry but I'm going to a party on
   Friday evening. How about lunch on Saturday?

week 37

Monday
   1 – 2.30 guitar lesson
   8 – 10 pm theatre club/play rehearsal

Tuesday
   12.30 lunch with Susan
   after 4 pm new washing machine arriving

Wednesday
   2 – 2.30 dentist
   8 – 10 pm play rehearsal

Thursday
   8.00 dinner at Renzo's restaurant
   mum and dad's Wedding Anniversary
   – don't forget flowers!

Friday
   A.M. all morning – do shopping for
                      weekend trip

Saturday
   7am sailing trip
   7am leave (NB don't forget Paul)

Sunday Back at around 10 pm

ENGLISH IN ACTION

You have the chance to lead a new country of about 75,000 people. Form a political party and prepare your ideas for an election.

1 Work in groups. Read about your country. List the six most important issues your party will work on, in order of importance.

Your country used to be a poor part of a bigger, wealthier country. It has no independent army and no prisons. 30% of the people cannot read or write. Schools exist in big towns only. There are ten hospitals in the whole country and only one doctor per 5,000 people. Many people are hungry. Rich foreign businessmen are interested in developing the land. They believe there is oil and the possibilities for agriculture are great. The climate is good and the countryside is beautiful. There is no airport but roads and local transport are good – they are old, however. There is very little entertainment for the people, no cinemas, theatres or community centres of any sort. Most people have televisions but few other luxury items. People are excited by the idea of change and think there will be rapid progress.

2 People living in your society will have certain responsibilities and rights. Decide on three things you can promise them and five basic laws. What will you do if they break the law?

3 Now, give your party an identity.

1 Choose a name, a leader and an advertising slogan.
2 Decide on a programme of events for the next month. Plan a number of meetings, social occasions and money-raising events.
3 Make a notice to advertise your first public meeting. Say where/what time you are having it and what arrangements you have made for food/drink, etc.

4 Hold your meeting. Tell people:

a) what you would like to do to improve the country.
b) what you can promise them.
c) what they will have to do in return.
d) the arrangements for the next month.

5 When you have heard all the political parties, hold an election. Vote for the best party.

Language review 13

1 Subject and object questions

Who/What can be the subject or the object of a question.

Subject	Object
Zoe likes Carlos. Who likes Carlos?	Zoe likes Carlos. Who does Zoe like?
(*Who* is the subject. *Carlos* is the object.)	(*Who* is the object. *Zoe* is the subject.)

a **Read this text. Make subject or object questions about the story. Use the words below.**

Mike arrived home at 9 o'clock. All the lights were on. A young man ran past Mike towards the front door. Mike stopped him but the man hit him. Mike fell to the floor. The man ran out of the door. Mike phoned the police. When the police arrived, Mike told them what had happened. The police started looking for the young man immediately.

Example: Who/arrive/home at 9 pm? – Who arrived home at 9 pm?

1 What/he/find?
2 Who/run/past/Mike?
3 What/Mike/do?
4 What/young man/do?
5 Who/fall/floor?
6 Who/run out/door?
7 Who/phone/police?
8 What/Mike/tell/police?
9 Who/police/look for/immediately?

b **Now give short answers to your questions.**

Example: Who arrived home at 9 o'clock? – Mike.

2 *Will/won't* (promises)

(I promise)	I'*ll* help you. I *won't* be late.

Promises are often combined with time clauses like *when/as soon as* **or conditions like** *if.*

Will	+ time expression	+ present form
I'*ll* help you	when	
	as soon as	I can.
	if	

c **Put the words in these promises in the correct order.**

Example: get as dinner will soon I cook as home I
– I will cook dinner as soon as I get home

1 the at I will airport when phone I you arrive
2 your send if address information you the give I me will you
3 go late I if won't party home to come I the
4 as computer stop using I as tell will the you soon I
5 finish bed they watching will go when TV to they
6 help I get will as you as I soon there

3 Present Continuous (future arrangements)

The Present Continuous is used for arrangements which often involve other people and/or advance organisation.

Present Continuous	+ time adverbials
We'*re* meet*ing* Juan We *aren't* play*ing* tennis	on Thursday. this week.
What *are* you do*ing*	tonight?

d **Find and correct six mistakes to do with the Present Continuous in this conversation.**

A: Hi Brian! How are you?
B: Fine, fine. How are you?
A: Not too bad. Listen, what do you do this evening?
B: Not a lot. Actually, I'm probably haveing a quiet evening at home alone.
A: Why don't you come round to my house? I inviting a few friends over for dinner.
B: That's very kind of you but I'm quite tired and . . .
A: OK. How about tomorrow night?
B: Well, my brother comes here and we put up some new wallpaper in the living room.
A: OK. I'm helping you. What time shall I come?
B: About 8.00. Thanks a lot.

How old are these

How ageist are you? It's hard to believe, but there is a difference of 37 years between the youngest and oldest person in these photos; their average age is 38!

Nikki Thompson

A make-up artist for top photographers, Nikki loves going to the cinema and going out with her six-year-old daughter, Kobe. Her suggestion for keeping good looks is to drink plenty of water. On being thirty five? 'It's the best time of my life: I am so much more secure than when I was younger.' Her philosophy: live one day at a time.

Sophie Norton

TV actress Sophie loves taking photographs or cooking delicious meals for friends. She keeps her good looks by swimming regularly. On being her age? 'Age is immaterial . I don't dress, think or act like a forty-year-old.' Her philosophy: friends are more important than anything else. Having young friends keeps you young.

Georgia Downs

Photographer Georgia says she tries to look after herself. ' I'm not always the best advertisement for healthy living, but I do aerobics. I run and I put night cream under my eyes!' she laughs. Georgia loves art galleries, photographic exhibitions and antique shops. On being twenty one? 'It's the perfect age; I enjoy it.' Her philosophy: smile and the world smiles with you!

people?

Tom Conti

Actor Tom says he does nothing special to keep his good looks but finally admits 'If anything, it's the work – the fantastic mental agility that goes with acting.' He also admits he has stopped drinking a glass of wine every evening. He now only has a glass with Sunday lunch – and the occasional cognac. In fact he loves good food and drink and has an ultra-healthy Mediterranean diet, based on pasta and olive oil. 'I eat Italian food almost exclusively and never use any fat other than olive oil for cooking.'

Alistair Blair

Designer Alistair looks as good as his own models. He loves good clothes and is dedicated to exercise. 'I enjoy running very much but can only find time to do it occasionally, but I always do a twenty minute workout of sit-ups and press-ups at home each morning.' He watches the calories he eats and has only one meal a day, dinner or lunch. He never eats breakfast. He believes sleep is really important and at the weekend he often sleeps for a complete day.

Lucille Anderson

Mother of two and boutique owner, Lucille loves going to the ballet, opera and concerts. She is not prepared to suffer for her looks; she eats and drinks what she likes. Keeping busy is her beauty secret. 'The good thing about getting older is your friends do too. You really shouldn't worry about it' Her philosophy: everything in moderation.

From *New Woman*

1 Preparation

1 **Work with another student. What do you think? Which of these ages is young/middle-aged/old?**

15   25   35   45   55   65   75   85   95

2 **Look at the people in the article opposite. Their average age is 38. How old do you think each person is?**

3 **Now, check your answers on page 126.**

2 Reading

1 **Look at the article again. Read about three of the people who interest you most and complete the chart for each person.**

Name	Job	Activities/Interests	Secret of youth

2 **Talk to students who read about other people. Add their information to your chart.**

3 Speaking

1 **What do you think? How can people stay young? Say which of these things, in your opinion:**

a) you have to do.
b) you don't have to do, but you should do.
c) you shouldn't do.

- drink a lot of water
- exercise
- smoke
- drink a glass of wine a day
- have a lot of sleep
- dress in clothes for younger people
- eat a lot of fruit and vegetables
- work and play hard
- get married
- mix with younger people

Example: I think you have to drink a lot of water but you definitely shouldn't smoke.

2 **Add three other ideas to help you live longer. Tell a different group your ideas.**

4 Listening

1 Before you listen, match the expressions in column A to their meanings in column B.

A   B
1 to take (your) time   a) to start a more regular
2 to settle down   life
3 to turn away   b) to leave
4 to take it easy   c) to relax
5 to make a change   d) to do something slowly
6 to go away   e) to look in another
                              direction
                           f) to act so that something
                              becomes different

2 Use your mini-dictionary to check the pronunciation of the expressions in column A. Which word is generally stressed in these expressions?

3 Read the words of the song 'Father and Son' by Cat Stevens. Work with another student. Complete each gap with one of the expressions in column A.

4 📖 Listen and check your answers.

1 Which verses are sung by the father and which by the son?
2 Which verse is repeated? Which words change?

5 Listen and read the words again.

1 Are this father and son happy about their relationship? Why/Why not?
2 List the advice the father gives his son.
3 What is the problem from the son's point of view? What is his solution?

Father and Son

It's not time to (1) . . . , just relax (2) . . .
You're still young, that's your fault,
there's so much you have to know.
Find a girl, (3) . . . , if you want, you can marry;
look at me, I am old but I'm happy.

I was once like you are now,
and I know that it's not easy to be calm
when you've found something going on.
But (4) . . . , think a lot, think of everything you've got,
for you will still be here tomorrow but your dreams may not.

How can I try to explain? When I do, he (5) . . . again.
It's always been the same, same old story.
From the moment I could talk, I was ordered to listen,
now there's a way, and I know that I have to (6) . . . .
I know I have to go!

It's not time to (7) . . . , just sit down, take it slowly.
You're still young, that's your fault,
there's so much you have to go through.
Find a girl, (8) . . . , if you want, you can marry;
look at me, I am old but I'm happy.

All the times that I've cried, keeping all the things I knew inside.
It's hard, but it's harder to ignore it.
If they were right, I'd agree, but it's them they know, not me.
Now there's a way, and I know that I have to (9) . . .
I know I have to go.

Cat Stevens 1970

5 Grammar

Shouldn't/mustn't/don't have to

The son hears:	The father means:
You *must* listen.	You *should* listen.
You *mustn't* go away.	You *shouldn't* go away.

1 Look at the sentences in the box above and answer these questions.

1 Which word is used to give advice, *should* or *must*?

2 Which word is used to give orders, *should* or *must*?

3 Is *must* similar in meaning to *should* or *have to*?

2 🔊 Listen and repeat the sentences above.

1 Which word has got main stress in each sentence?

2 How are *should* and *must* pronounced in these sentences? Can you hear the /t/ sound at the end of *shouldn't* and *mustn't*?

Listening

1 🔊 Listen to three people talking about age laws in the USA.

1 How many are American? How many are British?

2 What state are they talking about – California, Utah or New York?

3 What is special about this state?

2 Before you listen again, work with another student. Complete these sentences with *don't have to*, *shouldn't* or *mustn't*.

Example: Mormons *shouldn't* smoke or drink alcohol.

1 Mormons . . . drink tea or coffee.

2 Mormons . . . be vegetarians.

3 Men . . . have more than one wife.

4 A Mormon . . . marry another Mormon.

5 People . . . get married before they are 14.

6 When people are 18, they . . . get permission from parents to marry.

7 They . . . leave school before they are 16.

8 Men . . . go into the army when they leave school.

3 Now listen again and check your answers.

6 Speaking

Discuss with other students:

1 What are the age laws in your country for: a) smoking? b) alcohol? c) marriage? d) films you can/can't see? e) places children can/can't go? f) military service?

2 What do you think? When are you too young to do these things? When are you old enough to decide for yourself?

7 Writing

	They can leave school when they are 16	*but*	they don't have to.
Although	they can leave school when they are 16,		they don't have to.
	They can leave school when they are 16.	*However,*	

1 Look at the examples above and discuss with another student.

1 Where can *but/although/however* go in a sentence?

2 When do you need a full stop or a comma?

2 Complete this paragraph about laws affecting young people in Britain. Use *but*, *although* or *however*.

Education is compulsory between the ages of 5 and 16 (1) . . . many children begin school earlier with nursery school. (2) . . . they can leave school at 16, they have to stay longer if they want a good job or to go to university. There is no compulsory military service in Britain (3) . . . young people can volunteer and join the army when they are 16. (4) . . . they can't vote until they are 18, they can marry when they are 16. (5) . . ., until they are 18, they still need their parents' permission.

3 Write a similar paragraph about your country.

NB *mustn't* vs *don't have to*

a) You mustn't drink.

b) You don't have to drink.

Which means *you can if you want to*, a) or b)?

You are going to write a poem about a particular time of life.

1 📼 **First, read and listen to the poems on this page and answer these questions.**

1 What have the two poems got in common?
2 Which is more positive/negative?
3 Which do you like best? Why?

2 Listen again. Which words are stressed?

3 Say the poems to another student. Is the important information clear?

Prepare to write your poem individually, in pairs or in groups.

4 Choose two times of life to write about: babyhood, childhood, teenage, twenties, thirties, middle-age or old-age.

1 Write the name of each time of life on a different piece of paper.
2 For each time of life, what things do you think of? Below the name of each time, write:
   a) five or six adjectives.
   b) five or six verbs in the *-ing* form.
   c) five or six nouns.

Organise some of your words to make a 'Diamond poem'.

5 📼 **Listen to the instructions and write words in the spaces of the diamond below.**

LINE 1	___
LINE 2	___ ___
LINE 3	___ ___ ___
LINE 4	___ ___ ___ ___
LINE 5	___ ___ ___
LINE 6	___ ___
LINE 7	___

6 Read your poem. Make changes if necessary.

7 Listen to other poems. Which poems do you like best?

And the days are not full enough

And the days are not full enough
And the nights are not full enough
And life slips by like a field mouse
          Not shaking the grass.

Ezra Pound

Children

Children sleep at night
Children never wake up
When morning comes
Only the old ones wake up
Old Trouble is always awake

Children can't see over their eyes
Children can't hear beyond their ears
Children can't know outside of their heads

The old ones see
The old ones hear
The old ones know
The old ones are old.

Laura Riding

Language review 14

1 Shouldn't/mustn't/don't have to

These words express degrees of obligation.

Shouldn't + verb	It is not a good idea	
Mustn't + verb	It is important not	to do it.
Don't/Doesn't have to + verb	It is not necessary	

You've got a cold. You *don't have to go* to work but you can if you want to.
You've got the flu. You *shouldn't go* to work because others could catch it.
You've got a serious illness. You *mustn't go* to work because it's dangerous.

a For each of the sentences below, who do you think is speaking? Choose from these ideas.

parent to child   teacher to pupil   friend to friend
doctor to patient   boss to secretary

Example: You shouldn't smoke so much. – *friend to friend*

1 You mustn't run in the corridors.
2 You don't have to finish those letters until tomorrow.
3 You shouldn't watch so much TV. It isn't good for you.
4 You mustn't drink or drive while you are taking these tablets.

b Complete these sentences with *mustn't* or *doesn't/don't have to*.

1 I . . . get up early but I usually do.
2 You . . . drink and drive. It's dangerous.
3 You . . . tell anyone what I said. It's a secret.
4 She . . . wear a suit to work but she prefers to.
5 You . . . arrive late. It's an important meeting.

2 Too/enough + adjectives

Too + adjective expresses a problem.
Adjective + *enough* expresses as much as is necessary.
I can't drink this tea. It's *too* hot.
I can drink this tea. It's cool *enough*.

c Write sentences with *too*.

Example: I can't buy that car. It's *too expensive*.

1 I can't get the table through the door. It's . . .
2 I can't lift this box. It's . . .
3 I don't like shopping on Saturdays. It's . . .
4 She can't vote yet. She's . . .

d Write sentences with *enough*.

Example: I'm not going to buy it. It's not *cheap enough*.

1 I don't like travelling by coach. It's not . . .
2 He can't drive yet. He's not . . .
3 I don't want to swim in the sea. It's not . . .

3 Although/but/however

These words link opposing ideas but the word order and punctuation is different.

	He is intelligent	but	
Although	he is intelligent,		he can't get a job.
	He is intelligent.	However,	

e Connect sentences in column A with sentences in column B. Write three sentences for each example using *although*, *but* and *however*.

Example: Although it was raining, we went to the beach./It was raining but . . .

A	B
It was raining.	She bought a new jacket.
I passed my exam.	The pay was terrible.
She didn't have much money.	We couldn't find him.
We looked for him for ages.	We went to the beach.
It was an interesting job.	I decided not to go to university.

15 Consolidation

1 Across cultures: attitudes to children

Revises
Vocabulary: *But/although/however/and/or/so/because*
Grammar: *Have to/don't have to/mustn't/should/shouldn't*

1 Talk to other students about children in your country/family. Which of these things do/don't they have to do?

a) obey their parents without question
b) be very polite to adults
c) go to bed early
d) be quiet when their father is home
e) help with the housework/younger brothers and sisters
f) ask permission to get down from the table
g) ask permission to go out
h) ask for money if they want to buy something
i) other . . .

2 🖭 Listen to three children talking about their family life. Complete the chart below.

	Tessa	Manuel	Sarah
Their age			
Where they live			
Their nationality			
How strict they think their parents are			

3 Listen again. For each child, list what they:

a) have to do.
b) don't have to do.
c) mustn't do.

4 Compare your answers with another student.

5 Work with other students. Read these statements. Which do you agree/disagree with?

1 Children shouldn't be allowed in restaurants at night.
2 Every family should have a maximum of three children.
3 One parent should always be at home when the children are young.
4 Children should let parents live with them when they are old.
5 Boys and girls should be brought up in exactly the same way.
6 Children should have a special bedtime.

6 Choose one of the subjects you discussed above. Write a short article for an international magazine for parents, explaining what you think. Use words like *however/but/although/and/or/because/so* to link your ideas.

Should you SMACK children?

The hard facts about smacking

The Child Development Research Unit at Nottingham University interviewed 700 British mothers when their children were 1, 4, 7, and 11 years old. The results show that smacking is common in families from all social classes, decreasing as the child gets older.

How old?

- 62 per cent of mothers smack their baby before he is 1 year old.
- 68 per cent of mothers smack their 4-year-old child up to six times a week.
- 33 per cent of mothers smack their 7-year-old at least once a week.
- 15 per cent of mothers smack their 11-year-old child at least once a week.

Why?

- 67 per cent of 4-year-olds are smacked because they disobey rules, 38 per cent because they tell lies, and 58 per cent because they hit their mother.

Where?

Smacking is common among parents in other countries too. A survey of over

> *"My husband and I disagree about smacking. He is against it, he's not at home with the children all day."*
>
> *"If you find you are in danger of losing control with your child, you should leave the room. A smack should be given in anger - but not in fury - that's the distinction."*
>
> *"I don't mind a quick slap with the hand but when Dad uses his belt it's no joke!"*

3,000 sets of parents in America revealed that 90 per cent of 3-year-olds and 34 per cent of 15 to 17-year-olds are smacked on a regular basis. Research in Australia found that 81 per cent of boys and 74 per cent of girls at primary school are smacked by their parents. The same pattern is found in many other countries, including New Zealand.

But the fact that smacking is widespread doesn't make it right. That is why some countries now have laws forbidding parents from smacking their children; Finland, Denmark and Norway have all followed Sweden whose Parliament approved a bill in 1979 saying:

> *"Children are to be treated with respect for their person and individuality and may not be subjected to corporal punishment or any other humiliating treatment."*

> *"I will use the cane or the slipper on girls if they fail to do their homework."*

Adapted from Practical Parenting

---

2 Language in context: corporal punishment

Revises
Vocabulary: Countries; numbers
Grammar: Superlatives; *should/shouldn't*

1 Look at the quotes in the article above about smacking children.

1 Who said each one? Was it a teacher, a parent, a government, a child psychologist or a child?
2 Which of these things do they mention smacking children with: a belt, a slipper, a hand, a cane, a wooden spoon?

2 Now read the complete article and do the tasks below.

1 Complete the graphs.
2 What age child is smacked most often/least often?
3 Find the names of countries where smacking is:
   a) usual?   b) illegal?

3 Discuss these questions with other students.

1 Should parents/teachers smack naughty children?
2 Should parents punish children for these things? If so, how?

- coming home late
- doing something dangerous
- breaking things
- telling lies
- swearing
- smoking
- fighting

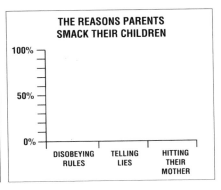

3 Thinking about learning: improving your memory

Revises
Vocabulary: Selected nouns; numbers; the time; dates; politics
Grammar: Past Continuous (interrupted action); Present Continuous (future arrangements); infinitive of purpose; subject and object questions; Present Perfect (unfinished past); *will* (promises); *as soon as* + Present Simple

visuals and rhymes

A TEST YOUR MEMORY

Look at this list for two minutes. Try to remember which word goes with each number.

6	soldier
8	diary
2	pet
9	poem
3	ice-cream
10	camera
7	map
4	princess
1	newspaper
5	father

Now turn to page 124 and complete the test.

B WOULD YOU MAKE A GOOD WITNESS?

You are in a bank when a robbery takes place.
Look at this picture for two minutes. Then answer the questions on page 125.

C SEE CONNECTIONS AND LEARN PATTERNS BY HEART

Put these sentences in pairs and make short dialogues.
Example: 1-B

1 What are you doing this evening?

2 I'm having dinner with Peter tomorrow.

3 Can you come to the cinema later?

4 Are you free at a quarter to seven?

A No, sorry. I'm having an early night.

B Nothing. Why?

C Yes, I am.

D Oh, give him my love.

Check your answers with a partner. Learn one or two of the dialogues by heart, then practise and continue the dialogues together.

D LEARN RHYMES BY HEART

Read this traditional rhyme and answer the question at the end.
Then listen to the rhyme and learn it by heart. Try the puzzle on people who are not in your class.

As I was going to St Ives,
I met a man with seven wives.
Each wife had seven sacks,
Each sack had seven cats,
Each cat had seven kits.

Kits, cats, sacks and wives,
How many were going to St Ives?

15

Puzzles to keep your *mind active*

A TIME GAME

Imagine you are looking in a mirror. Your clock appears to say half past ten. Is the real time:

half past four ?   half past seven ?
half past ten ?   half past one ?

B WORD GAME

Make other words of three or more letters from the word below. Who can make the most?

PARLIAMENTARY

lamp
men

C CHAIN GAME

Play a chain game, saying why you went to market. Each person remember what went before and add to the list alphabetically.

I went to market to get an apple.

I went to market to get an apple and a banana.

D IMPROVE YOUR GENERAL KNOWLEDGE

Match the questions to the names and dates.

Questions

1 a Who said 'I want to be alone'?
  b When did she/he say it ?
2 a Who invented the telephone?
  b When did she/he invent it?
3 a Who designed the first bikini?
  b When did she/he design it?
4 a Who wrote *Frankenstein*?
  b When did she/he write it?
5 a Who made the first pair of jeans?
  b When did she/he make them?

Answers

Names	Dates
Levi Strauss	1946
Mary Shelley	1932
Louis Reard	1876
Greta Garbo	1818
Alexander Graham Bell	1946

E THINK IMAGINATIVELY

Look at the photograph below with another student. Answer these questions imaginatively.

1 What is the couple's relationship?
2 How long have they known each other?
3 How long have they lived in this house?
4 What are their jobs? How long have they had them?
5 What has just happened?
6 What are they doing this evening?

F FEEL RELAXED - IT HELPS YOU LEARN!

Look at this list of relaxing activities. Choose four things which make you feel good. Add one other.

• having a bath
• listening to music
• wearing expensive perfume
• buying a bunch of flowers
• phoning a friend
• watching TV
• going to the cinema
• eating chocolate
• other?

Reward yourself for your hard work. Make five promises to yourself.

Example: As soon as I get home, I'll have a bath. Then, I'll ...

16 | *How much is too much?*

Animals; adjectives for describing people (4);
want + object + infinitive

1 Preparation

1 **Work with another student. Find and name ten animals hidden in the picture.**

2 **Use your mini-dictionary on page 138 to check the meaning and pronunciation of these adjectives.**

brave   intelligent   faithful
dirty   independent   sly
cruel   affectionate   vain
stupid

Say what animals you associate with each word.

2 Speaking

1 **Work with other students. Look at the pictures of Aesop's fable *The Fox and the Crow* below. Tell the story from the pictures.**

2 **Now, answer these questions.**

  1 Which adjective from the list above best describes the fox/ crow?
  2 What is the moral of the story?

3 Grammar: *want* + object + infinitive

> a) The fox *wants to drop* the cheese.
> b) The fox *wants the crow to drop* the cheese.

1 **Look at the sentences above and answer these questions.**

  1 Who will drop the cheese in sentence a)/sentence b)?
  2 What pronoun could replace *the crow/the cheese*?

2 **Make sentences about the story using the prompts below.**

Example: The fox wants/drop the piece of cheese. – The fox wants the crow to drop the piece of cheese.

  1 The fox wants/eat the piece of cheese.
  2 The fox wants/sing a song.
  3 The fox doesn't want/swallow the piece of cheese.
  4 The fox wants/open its mouth.
  5 The crow wants/eat the piece of cheese.
  6 The crow wants/show off its beautiful voice.
  7 The crow doesn't want/eat the piece of cheese.
  8 The crow wants/flatter it more.

What a beautiful bird! I am sure you sing beautifully too!

Time expressions: *when, as soon as, after, before,* *who* in relative clauses; *a* vs *the*

5 Listening

1 🖿 **Listen to a traditional song, 'I know an old lady who swallowed a fly', and answer these questions.**

1 Which animals in the picture are in the song?
2 What did the woman do to the animals?
3 How did she die?

2 Work with another student. Take it in turns to ask about each animal in the song, like this:

A: Why did she swallow the spider?
B: To catch the fly.

6 Grammar: relative clauses

> a) I know an old lady. She swallowed a fly.
> b) I know an old lady *who* swallowed a fly.

1 Look at the examples above and answer these questions.

1 Which word in sentence b) links the two sentences in a)?
2 Which word does it replace in a)?

2 Work with another student. Write sentences about interesting people you know.

Example: STUDENT A: I know someone who has cycled across India!
STUDENT B: I know someone who can speak six languages!

3 Tell other students about the people you know. Who knows the most interesting person?

> **NB** *a* vs *the*
>
> a) A lady swallowed a fly.
> b) The lady died.
>
> 1 Do we use *a* or *the* to introduce a subject?
> 2 Do we use *a* or *the* to talk about the same subject again?

4 Writing

1 Work with another student and write the story together.

a) Begin like this: One day a crow was flying past an open window when . . .

b) Use time expressions like these to make the story more interesting.

When	
As soon as	the fox said this, the crow . . .
After	
Before	

2 Read other students' stories. Give suggestions to make them clearer.

7 Vocabulary: products/packages

1 Look at the list of products below with another student. Answer these questions.

1 Which four products don't you eat or drink?
2 Which of these things do/don't *you* need to buy?

toothpaste	chocolate	coffee	soap
tomato paste	tomatoes	soup	water
mayonnaise	matches	sugar	cake
marmalade	biscuits	milk	jam
cigarettes	cheese	wine	tea

2 Use each expression below once only to identify things in the photograph.

a piece *of cheese*   a packet of . . .
a can/tin of . . .   a jar of . . .
a tube of . . .   a box of . . .
a bar of . . .   a bottle of . . .

Pronunciation

1 🔲 Listen and check your answers.

1 Is main stress on the food or the package?
2 How do you pronounce *a* and *of*?

2 Listen again and repeat, like this:

/s əv/
a piece of cheese

3 Talk to two other students. Look at the list of products again. Which package can each product go in?

Example: Toothpaste can go in a tube.

4 🔲 Listen to some British people doing the last exercise. Are your answers the same?

5 Name one other thing that comes in each package.

8 Grammar: *much/many/a lot*

How *many cans* of soup are there?	*A lot.*
How *many boxes* of matches are there?	*Not many.*
How *many matches* are there in each box?	*A lot.*
How *much soup* is there in each can?	*Not much.*

1 Look at the examples above and answer these questions.

1 Which of these are countable nouns? Which are uncountable nouns?

cans   boxes   matches   soup

2 Do we ask *How much* . . . or *How many* . . . with countable/uncountable nouns?
3 Do we generally use *much/many* in positive or negative answers?
4 When do we use *a lot*?

2 Write questions to ask another student about things they have done this week. Use the ideas below and *How much/How many*?

Example: films/see? How many films have you seen?

. . . wine/drink?
. . . clothes/buy?
. . . English homework/do?
. . . times/phone parents?
. . . television/watch?
. . . books/read?
. . . money/spend?

3 Ask another student your questions. Answer with *a lot*, *not much*, *not many* or *none* and then explain in more detail.

Example: A: How many films have you seen this week?
         B: Not many, only two. I usually see at least three.

> **NB** *much/many* and money
>
> *How much* money have you spent?
> *How many* dollars is that?
>
> The word *money* is uncountable in English. Are *pounds*, *francs*, *yen* and *dinars* countable or uncountable?

Chocomania!!

omic year area

- Every year the British eat nearly half a million tons of chocolate. This costs nearly £4 billion. That is about 20lb for every person in Britain. The Italians only eat about 3lb of chocolate a year.
- Chocolate contains a chemical which is the same one as the brain produces when we fall in love. It also contains such strong stimulants that a race horse who ate a Mars bar before a race failed a drug test.

- British chocolate is thought not to be as good as Swiss chocolate but much better than American chocolate. This is so poor that it is not called chocolate but candy.
- Generally speaking, the more expensive chocolate is, the fewer the calories there are.
- There are five million 'chocoholics' in Britain, that is, people who eat more than six bars of chocolate a week.

Telenhone con

From *The Sunday Correspondent*

9 Reading

1 Before you read, answer these questions.

1 Which of the chocolate bars in the photograph do you have in your country?
2 What other chocolate bars can you buy in your country?
3 How much chocolate do you think you eat a week?
4 What is a *chocoholic*?

2 Read the sentences below. What do you think? Is a), b) or c) correct?

1 British people eat:
  a) more chocolate than Italians.
  b) less chocolate than Italians.
  c) the same amount of chocolate as Italians.
2 When we eat a lot of chocolate we:
  a) feel loved.
  b) feel unloved.
  c) feel in love.
3 The best chocolate is considered to be:
  a) British chocolate.
  b) Swiss chocolate.
  c) American chocolate.
4 Cheap chocolate has:
  a) more calories than expensive chocolate.
  b) fewer calories than expensive chocolate.
  c) the same number of calories as expensive chocolate.
5 You are a chocoholic if you eat:
  a) five bars of chocolate a week.
  b) six bars of chocolate a week.
  c) seven bars of chocolate a week.

3 Now read the article. Were your answers to the questions in the last exercise correct? Do any of the answers surprise you?

Listening

1 🖵 Listen to a chocoholic and answer the questions below.

1 Does she want to stop her addiction?
2 What would her husband like her to do?
3 What would she like him to do?

2 Listen again and answer these questions.

1 When does she eat chocolate?
2 How does it affect her family?
3 What three things show that she is a chocoholic?
4 What effect does it have on her health?

NB Weight in *lbs* and *kgs*

A pound (lb) is 5/8 of a kilo (kg).

Is a 2lb box of chocolates heavier or lighter than a 2kg box of chocolates?

| Thomas Cook | Foreign Exchange | | | |

| FOREIGN CURRENCY NOTES | | | TRAVELLER'S CHEQUES | |
WE BUY	WE SELL		WE BUY	WE SELL
			2.99	2.25
2.99	2.23	AUSTRALIA		
18.58	17.29	AUSTRIA		
54.39	50.68	BELGIUM		
2.17	2.01	CANADA	2.15	2.02
8.96	8.36	FRANCE	8.91	8.38
2.64	2.47	GERMANY	2.62	2.47
329	302	GREECE		
2.97	2.78	HOLLAND	2.95	2.78
13.57	12.55	HONG KONG	13.49	12.58
1.03	.93	REP. OF IRELAND		
2244	2051	ITALY		
.59	.52	MALTA		
231	210	PORTUGAL		
177	166	SPAIN	176	166
2.30	2.15	SWITZERLAND	2.29	2.15
1.77	1.64	USA	1.79	1.64
3	2	COMMISSION RATE	3	2
2.50	2.00	MINIMUM CHARGE	3.00	3.00

You are in an English bank.

1 Look at the chart above. How many pounds sterling will you get for:

100 French francs?   2,000 Greek drachmas?
300 German marks?   200 American dollars?

You are going to travel from Britain to one

of the countries in the chart.

2 Choose where you want to go.

3 You have got sterling to change. Complete this conversation with the bank clerk.

BANK CLERK: Can I (1) . . . you?
YOU: Yes, please. I'd like to (2) . . . some money.
BANK CLERK: What currency would you like (3) . . . buy?
YOU: (4) . . .
BANK CLERK: That's no problem.
YOU: How much will I get (5) . . . £100?
BANK CLERK: (6) . . . How would you like it? In large or small notes?
YOU: (7) . . ., please.

4 Practise the conversation in pairs.

You need to do some other things

at the bank.

5 What do you think? How do you ask to:

a) open a current account?
b) apply for a credit card?
c) speak to the manager?
d) arrange a transfer?
e) cash a cheque?

6 ▭ Listen to another customer. Which of the things above does she want to do? Which does she actually do?

7 Use this customer's completed cheque as a model. Copy the blank cheque into your notebook and write a cheque for £100 to cash at the bank.

8 Now write a cheque from your account for your partner!

Language Review 16

1 Verbs: *want* (someone) *to do* something

Want (*need* and *would like*) can be followed by the object + infinitive structure.

Subject	+ *want/would like/ need*	+ (object pronoun)	+ infinitive
I/You We/They	want would like	(you)	to help.
She/He/(It)	needs		

a Put the words in these sentences in the correct order.

Example: wants to some you she and go buy milk. – She wants you to go and buy some milk.

1 need computer to the do use you now?
2 you for exercise finish this I to want homework.
3 international would to I bank like work an for.
4 do what do want you to me?
5 tonight go you to want out do?
6 book would lend you you that me to like?
7 home need us they them take to.
8 him me help to does want he?

2 *Who* in relative clauses

You can use *who* to join two sentences about the same person.

I know a man. *He* has got six children.
I know a man *who* has got six children.

b Join the sentences on the left to the sentences on the right, using *who*. Use each sentence once only.

Example: He was a young man *who* liked to play football.

She is a selfish person.	They had the same idea.
He was a young man.	She likes meeting people.
There were a lot of people.	He had short, black hair.
She is a very friendly person.	He liked to play football.
My teacher was the person you saw.	She always does what she wants.

3 A *lot/much/many* + uncountable or plural countable nouns

	+ Uncountable noun		+ Plural countable noun	
Positive	I have got	a lot of	coffee and	a lot of	apples.
Negative	I haven't got	much	coffee or	many	apples.
Question	Have you got	much	coffee or	many	apples?

c Seven of these sentences are incorrect. Mark them correct (C) or incorrect (I).

Example: I haven't got many time but can I see your new goldfish? (I)

1 There are not much animals that I don't like.
2 A lot people like dogs but I don't.
3 Cats are much work.
4 I haven't got much friends but my pets keep me company.
5 Not many animals are more independent than the cat.
6 I've got a lot of chickens. I keep them in the garden.
7 You haven't given the cats very many food.
8 There is much work to do.
9 They haven't got much money left after the holiday.
10 How many fruit did you buy?

d Correct the incorrect sentences.

Example: I haven't got *much* time but can I see your new goldfish?

Present Simple passive

1 Preparation

1 Name the items above. Where are they made/produced?

Example: Tartan scarves are made in Scotland.

2 Discuss with another student. Where are the products below made/produced?

Seiko watches   Scotch whisky   Audi cars
Gucci bags   Lindt chocolate   Persian rugs

> **NB** *make vs are made*
>
> a) The Japanese *make* Seiko watches.
> b) Seiko watches *are made* in Japan.
>
> 1 What seems more important in sentence a), the Japanese or the watches?
> 2 What seems more important in sentence b), Japan or the watches?

2 Reading

1 Read the headline of the newspaper article. Why does it catch the reader's attention?

2 Write questions with two other students. What would you like to know when you read the article?

3 Tell the class your questions. Add other students' questions to your list.

4 Read the article. How many of your questions are answered?

viduals from 26 to 20. Wo...

The man who died twice

THE MYSTERY OF THE man who died twice should be solved today when his wife identifies his body.

A man calling himself Clive Reed was found dead in the Cuillin mountains in Scotland last Thursday. Three-quarters of a mile away the body of his friend, Miss Hilary Wells, 26, of Oxford, was found.

When the police checked Mr Reed's papers they realised his real name was Mr Clive Greenwood from Pembury High Street near Tunbridge Wells who was missing, presumed drowned, after his clothes were found on a cliff top near Durdle Door, Dorset, last April.

Identified? Clive Greenwood

From *The Evening Standard*

3 Speaking

**1 What do you think? Discuss these questions
with other students.**

1 Why did Mr Greenwood go to Scotland?
2 How did he meet Miss Hilary Wells?
3 What was their relationship?
4 How exactly did she die?
5 How did he die?

> Do you think they went there together?

> Yes, I think so because . . .

> No, I don't think so because . . .

**2 Tell other groups what your group thinks. Listen
to other students. Say why you think their ideas
are possible/impossible. Can you agree on a final
version?**

**3 Turn to page 126. Read a later newspaper article
about the same story and answer these
questions.**

1 Where was your story correct/incorrect?
2 What are the answers to the five questions in
exercise 1 above?

**4 Read the article on page 126 again and find a
word that means:**

1 to take a person out of danger. (*v.*) (line 3)
2 not to succeed. (*v.*) (line 4)
3 to look at a person/thing and say who/what
they are. (*v.*) (line 6)
4 to die in water. (*v.*) (line 8)
5 earlier. (*adj.*) (line 22)
6 to go away and not be seen. (*v.*) (line 24)
7 worth a lot of money. (*adj.*) (line 28)
8 worried. (*adj.*) (line 35)

4 Grammar: the passive

> a) Clive *found* Hilary's body.
> b) Clive's body *was found* in the mountains.

**1 Look at the sentences above and answer these
questions.**

1 Who found Hilary's body? Who found Clive's
body?
2 Is the person who found the body important in
sentence a) or b)?
3 Why is the passive form *'was found'* used in
sentence b)?
4 How do you make the passive form of *find*:
a) in the Present Simple?
b) in the Past Simple?

**2 Complete the chart below. What do you notice
about the forms of the Past Simple and past
participles? Which verb is different?**

Present	Past Simple	Past participle
find	found	found
. . .	thought	thought
. . .	went	been/gone
meet	met	. . .
. . .	had	had
. . .	tried	tried
die	died	. . .
check	. . .	checked
tell	. . .	told

**3 Retell the story. Put the verbs in brackets in the
Past Simple active or passive form.**

1 Last April, Clive Greenwood's clothes (find)
were found on a cliff.
2 Everyone (think) . . . he was dead.
3 He (go) . . . to Scotland where he (meet) . . .
Hilary Wells.
4 Last week, she (have) . . . an accident in the
mountains.
5 Clive (try) . . . to get help.
6 He (die) . . . of the cold.
7 His body (find) . . . in the mountains, a mile
away from Hilary's.
8 His papers (check). . . by the police. They
realised who he was.
9 His wife (tell) . . .
10 She (go) . . . to Scotland to identify the body.

5 Speaking

Talk to other students and answer these questions.

1 How did these famous people die?
2 Who died of natural causes? Who committed suicide?
3 Who was murdered? Were they stabbed, shot or poisoned?

Example: Mao Tse Tung *died of natural causes.*

Mao Tse Tung . . .	John Lennon . . .	Julius Caesar . . .
Martin Luther King . . .	Napoleon . . .	Indira Gandhi . . .
Emperor Hirohito . . .	Marilyn Monroe . . .	President Kennedy . . .

6 Listening

1 🖭 **Listen to three people discussing their favourite people in history. For each person, complete the chart below.**

	Favourite person	Reasons
Person 1		
Person 2		
Person 3		

Grammar: *so* and *such*

> She was *so* beautiful.
> She was *such* a beautiful woman.

1 Look at the sentences above and answer these questions.

1 Which word goes before an adjective on its own, *so* or *such*?
2 Which word goes before a noun, with or without an adjective?
3 Do *so/such* make the adjective weaker or stronger?

2 Complete these sentences with *so* or *such*.

1 Indira Gandhi was . . . a respected person.
2 That's . . . an important thing for a politician.
3 Martin Luther King was . . . a gentle, non-violent man.
4 He was . . . sure he was right.
5 Marilyn Monroe was . . . an ordinary person with . . . big dreams.
6 She had . . . an unhappy life.
7 She was . . . beautiful and successful but . . . frightened and alone.
8 Her life was a disaster although she was in . . . a lot of successful films.

3 🖭 Listen, check your answers and repeat the sentences.

4 Tell another student about a politician, a film star or an ordinary person you admire.

1 What do/did they do?
2 What sort of person are/were they?
3 Why do you admire them?

7 Pronunciation: /s/, /z/, /ʃ/

> /z/ /s/ /ʃ/   /z/
> He was so sure he was right.

1 🖭 **Listen and repeat the sentence above about Martin Luther King.**

2 **Say the words below to another student. Put them in the correct column.**

/s/	/z/	/ʃ/
so	was	sure

sugar	bus	writes	choose
nose	use	lose	shoe
sometimes	sea	sock	strong
house	sell	easy	should

3 **Write a sentence including as many words with 's' as possible.**

4 **Read your sentence to other students. Try saying their sentences.**

5 **Read the puzzle below and answer the question.**

She sells sea shells
on the seashore.

How many 's's in that?

6 **Learn the puzzle to ask other people.**

RASPUTIN

the evil russian monk rasputin was seen as a bad influence on the russian royal family prince felix yussupov with three friends decided to kill him they invited him to a wild party in a cellar and fed the monk cakes and wine poisoned with cyanide unfortunately the victim was immune to cyanide to the horror of the murderers he continued eating and drinking happily finally the prince tried to shoot him but was stopped by the hypnotic eye of rasputin yussupov ran away rasputin tried to follow him but was shot stabbed and hit repeatedly his hands and feet were tied and finally he fell into the icy river neva it was afterwards discovered that his death was by drowning not poison or gunshot wounds

8 Writing

1 Work with another student. Which of the following begin with capital letters in English?

names of people	names of animals
things	days of the week
months of the year	seasons
nationalities	languages
countries	colours

2 Read this text to check your answers.

> Capitalisation sometimes causes problems for students of English. This is because many words begin with capital letters in English and don't in other languages. Examples include days of the week, months of the year and the names of nationalities and languages as well as countries. Names of people begin with capital letters but not names of things, colours, animals or seasons which begin with small letters. 'That's illogical,' I hear German students shout. 'Why don't names of things also begin with capital letters?' Don't ask me! I never said English was logical!

3 Match the punctuation marks to their names. When are they used in the text in the last exercise?

Name	Mark
a comma	.
an apostrophe	" "
a question mark	,
a full stop	?
an exclamation mark	'
speech marks	!

4 Put capital letters and punctuation marks in the text about Rasputin above.

5 Now read the text and answer these questions.
  1 How did Rasputin die?
  2 Who tried to kill him. How? Why?

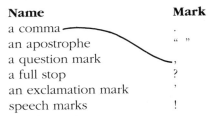

NB Passives + *by/with*

He was shot *by* the prince *with* a gun.

1 Who did the action?
2 What did he use?

ENGLISH IN ACTION

You are going to find out about the local history of the people and area where you study.

1 Choose one of these subjects to find out about.

- The town.
- Any famous people who come from the area.
- Local traditions, food, clothes, etc.
- The building/institution where you study.

2 Work with students who want to find out about the same subject.

1 List the questions you would like to ask.
2 Decide how you will get your information. Will you interview people, give them questionnaires or work in the local library?
3 Divide the work between you, if necessary.

Collect your information and report back.

3 Make a group poster to show other students what you found out.

1 Choose the headings, articles and pictures/photographs to use.
2 Decide where to put these things on your poster.
3 Make the poster.

4 Look at other students' posters. Ask them questions to get more information.

1 Verbs: Passive/active forms

Active verb forms stress the subject of a sentence.
Passive verb forms stress the object. (The subject is often unknown or unimportant to the speaker.)

	Active	Passive (*be* + past participle)
Present Simple	They *speak* English here.	English *is spoken* here.
Past Simple	They *built* it in 1867.	It *was built* in 1867.

In passive sentences, use:
by + person/thing to show who/what did the action.
He was hit *by a child*.

with + thing for the instrument used.
He was hit by a child *with a stick*.

a Write complete sentences using the Present Simple or Past Simple passive form.

Example: Our dog/find/police/Friday. – Our dog was found by the police on Friday.

1 I/meet/the airport/a friend/last night.
2 My bags/check/Customs Officers/the airport.
3 Wine/produce/the south of England.
4 The children/tell/story/before they went to bed.
5 All the food/the party/eat/before nine o'clock.
6 A large new hospital/open/the Queen/last weekend.
7 £100,000/steal/a bank in Birmingham/this morning.
8 The post/collect/9 am and 1 pm/every day.
9 A bell/ring/end/school/each day.
10 The policeman/hit/bottle/angry teenagers/yesterday evening.

2 I think/I don't think + so

If you use *so* in these expressions, you do not repeat the idea already expressed.

Question	Do you think	TV is a waste of time?
Positive	Yes, I think	so.
Negative	No, I don't think	so.

b Respond to these questions with *Yes, I'm sure*, *Yes, I think so*, *No, I don't think so* or *I've got no idea*.

Example: Is Mercury the nearest of the planets? – No, I don't think so.

1 Is Niagara Falls the highest waterfall in the world?
2 Are there 49 states in the United States of America?
3 Can the Great Wall of China be seen from space?
4 Was the Eiffel Tower once the tallest building in the world?
5 Did the famous artist El Greco come from Crete?
6 Do nearly one quarter of the world's population live in China?
7 Was the Statue of Liberty a present from Italy to America?
8 Did Karl Marx spend more than half his life in London?

3 So vs such

So and *such* give extra emphasis to an idea.
So is used before adjectives (without nouns).
Such is used before nouns (with or without adjectives).

She is *so* kind.
She is *such* a kind person.

c Complete the sentences. (There are different possible answers.)

1 I really liked him. He was so . . .
   He had such . . .
2 I'm sorry we went to that restaurant. It was so . . .
   It was such . . .
3 We had a great holiday. The weather was so . . .
   The people were so . . .
   The hotel was so . . .
4 Shall we buy that house? It's so . . .
   It's got such . . .
5 The party was fantastic! I had such . . .
   The people were so . . .

KITCHEN

BEDROOM

START

MURDER

Aim
To solve a murder by naming the murderer, the weapon and the room the murder was committed in.

Rules
1 Use a pack of game cards (including murderer cards, weapon cards and room cards).
2 Make a list of all possible:
   a) murderers (the players).
   b) weapons.
   c) rooms.
3 Without looking, choose three cards: one murderer card, one weapon card, one room card. Put them face down to one side. They are the solution to the murder.
4 Divide the other cards between the players. Tick (✓) your cards off your list of murderers, weapons and rooms.
5 Use dice and counters to move from room to room. Make accusations when you get to a room.

Example: *The murder was committed in the kitchen by Graziella with the gun.*

6 If other players show you a card you have mentioned, tick it off your list.
7 The winner is the first player to write down the complete and correct accusation.

BATHROOM

START

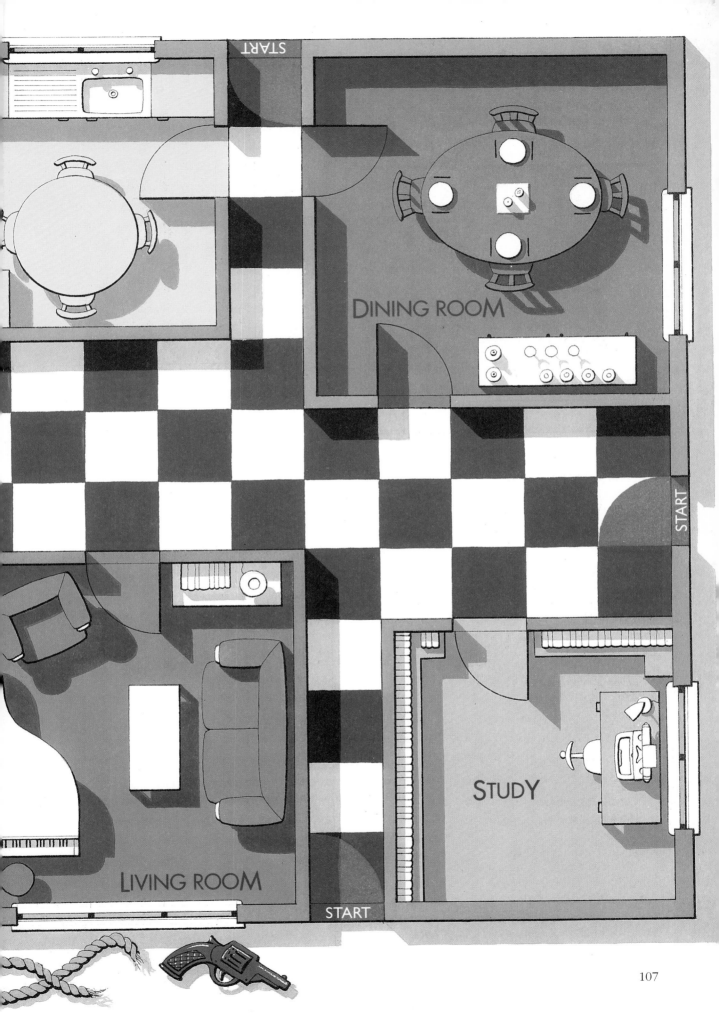

START

DINING ROOM

START

LIVING ROOM

START

STUDY

18 *What would you give up?*

Household equipment; *give up*; *would*
(speculation); *could* vs *would*

1 Preparation

**1 Look at the kitchen above
with another student.**

1 Which of the things below
can you see in the picture?
2 Which room do you
associate with the other things?

a telephone
a freezer
a video
a compact disc player
a radio
an electric kettle
an answer phone
a washing-machine/dryer
a dishwasher
a cooker
a microwave (oven)
a toaster
a fridge
a television
a computer
a stereo
a hairdryer

2 Talk to your partner.

1 Which of these things have
you got?
2 Imagine you had to live
without one of them. Which
would you give up? Which
wouldn't you give up?

Example: I'd give up the video
but I wouldn't give up the TV.

2 Grammar: *would* (speculation)

> I'*d* give up the video.
> I *wouldn't* give up the television.

1 Look at the sentences above and answer these questions.

1 Has this person given up her/his video?
2 Is this person doing the action or imagining the action?
3 What does '*d* stand for in *I'd give up*?
4 How do you make the question form with *would*? What are the
possible short answers?

2 Complete this dialogue with *would*, *wouldn't* or '*d*.

A: What . . . you do with £2,000?
B: I . . . buy a motorbike. . . . you do something different?
A: Yes, I . . . I . . . put it in the bank.
B: Oh, I . . . That's boring! I . . . spend it immediately. It . . . do
anything in the bank.
A: Yes, it . . . It . . . make lots of interest. Then I . . . buy a bigger,
better motorbike!

**3 Talk to two other students. Imagine you have to share a house.
You can only afford to buy eight of the household possessions in
Exercise 1 Preparation between you. What would you buy?**

> **NB** *could* vs *would*
>
> a) I *couldn't* live without a fridge.
> b) I *wouldn't* live without a fridge.
>
> 1 Which sentence suggests it is not possible to live without a
> fridge?
> 2 Which sentence suggests the speaker doesn't want to live
> without a fridge?

Goodbye to all that!

1 RACHEL

When Jim moved out of our flat and into the arms of another woman, he took everything - the bed, the sofa, the stereo, our entire collection of Elvis Presley records, cutlery, bathroom towels, sheets, the lot. 'That's OK,' I said, 'I can manage ...' But then I realised the phone was missing. I began to panic. How could I call my mother to tell her the good news (that Jim had gone)? How could I ring my friends to invite them over for a celebratory drink? How could the office contact me? How could I phone out for my regular Friday night pizza? My lifeline was cut.

Life was very busy over the next two weeks: at work, seeing friends, buying new things for my flat. And then I realised that I still didn't have a phone. In fact I started noticing some of the many advantages of not having a phone: no more ringing bells on Sunday mornings or in the middle of the night; no more wrong numbers; no more salesmen selling insurance; no more enormous telephone bills. Since then I've started writing letters again. It's great, you can keep a letter and read it again and again but you can't keep a phone call. I have also saved a lot of money on overseas phone calls. And my health has improved: I've stopped eating home-delivered junk food and started cooking good meals.

2 ROB

In 1987 on January 1st, I made a New Year's resolution that changed my life. I gave up my TV. Most of my friends couldn't believe it. They thought I must now be either mad, an intellectual or a snob. I like to think none of these are true. It wasn't easy to convince people I was serious; the television licensing authorities sent an inspector to check I really did not possess a TV. The interesting thing is that other people now feel the need to explain why they have a television. They say things like: 'Of course I only watch the news and the occasional film' or 'Well, we only have ours for the children.'

In fact, since then, a number of things have changed in my way of life. First of all, my wife and I have started talking much more. Before, we both came home from work, had something to eat and then collapsed in front of the TV until one of us fell asleep. Now we have more time generally and more time for each other. We have both started doing old hobbies again. Rita has begun playing the piano and I have started painting once more. Another major change is that we see friends a lot more often. All in all it's been a very positive change. I can't imagine we will ever go back.

From *New Woman*

3 Reading

1 Read the article above and answer these questions.

1 What have these people given up?
2 Has it had a positive or negative effect on their lives?

2 Read the article again. Answer these questions for each person.

1 Which occasion in the past made them give up their treasured possession?
2 In what way do they say it was difficult?
3 Name the things that have changed for the better in their lives.
4 What image do you get of how their lives used to be?

3 Choose five new words to learn from the article. Look them up in a dictionary and answer these questions for each word.

1 What do they mean?
2 How are they pronounced?
3 Write each word in a sentence to show what it means.

4 Speak to other students. Tell one another about the words you chose.

4 Speaking

1 Discuss what you think of television with other students. Use the ideas below and expressions like these:

> I don't really agree.

> I agree.

> I couldn't agree more.

- Television is bad for family life.
- It is a good way to learn a foreign language.
- Children can learn more from television than from reading.
- More people would go to the cinema if television was abolished.
- Programmes which are unsuitable for children should not be shown before 9 pm.
- There should be no control on television advertising.
- There would be less violence in a society with no television.

2 Tell the class what your group thought. How many people agreed/disagreed with the ideas above?

5 Writing

1 Look at the advertisements on this page from a health magazine.

1 Which one says it can help you give up unwanted habits?
2 What do the other advertisements offer?

2 Separate the two jumbled letters below and put them in order. One letter is to a friend and one is answering an advertisement.

3 Now, write to one of the advertisements to get more information.

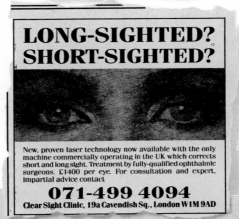

a. I saw your advertisement in the paper

b. Please give my best wishes to your family.

c. Yours faithfully,

d. I was so sorry to hear about your problem.

e. Dear Miranda,

f. I would be grateful for an early reply

g. Thank you for your letter.

h. Dear Sir/Madam,

i. With love from,

j. Please would you send me a copy of your information pack.

k. and would like to thank you in advance for your help.

l. I really want to help

m. and I would like to know more about your product.

n. so phone me and let's meet soon.

If + past + *would* (second conditional); types of music; *make (someone) feel* + adjective

6 Listening

1 🖵 **Listen to an interview with the actor Anthony Hopkins for the BBC radio programme, 'Desert Island Discs'. Each week a famous person chooses eight pieces of music they would take to a desert island.**

1 What musical instrument does Anthony Hopkins play?
2 Which dream did he give up when he was younger?
3 How did he choose the music to take with him?

2 🖵 **Listen to the end of the interview and complete his choices below. What would he take with him?**

Luxury . . .
Food . . .
Music – which would he most like to take?
   • 'Consolation No. 3' (Liszt)
   • 'Where the blue of the night' (Bing Crosby)
   • 'Myfanwy' (The Triorchy Male Voice Choir)
Book . . .

3 Imagine you had to go and live on the desert island. What music/luxury/food/book would you take? Take it in turns to interview your partner.

7 Grammar: *If* + past + *would*

> *If* I *went* to a desert island, *I'd* take a piano.

1 Look at the sentence above and answer these questions.

1 Is the situation real or imagined?
2 Is the situation in the past or the future?
3 What comes after *if,* a past or future form?

2 Answer these questions with your partner. In what situations would/wouldn't you do the following things?

Example: Would you steal a loaf of bread? – Yes, if I was hungry./No, not even if I was hungry.

1 Would you steal a loaf of bread? Yes, . . ./No, not even if . . .
2 Would you live permanently abroad?
3 Would you fight for your country?
4 Would you marry someone you didn't like?
5 Would you lie to the police?

3 Write the answers to these questions in full.

Example: I'd steal a loaf of bread if I was hungry.

8 Vocabulary: types of music

1 🖵 **Listen to the adjectives below which end in -ed. Are they pronounced /t/, /d/ or /ɪd/?**

depress<u>ed</u>   annoy<u>ed</u>   relax<u>ed</u>   romantic
frighten<u>ed</u>   excit<u>ed</u>   worri<u>ed</u>   nothing at all

2 🖵 **Listen to a possible selection of 'Desert Island Discs'. Number the type of music in the order you hear it.**

classical music . . .   pop music . . .   jazz . . .
folk music . . .   blues . . .   reggae . . .

3 Listen to the music again. Choose an adjective to say how each piece of music makes you feel.

4 Compare your answers with a partner.

Example: The classical music makes me feel relaxed. What about you?

5 Talk to other students. What type of music do most people in the class like best?

You and your partner enter a competition.

You, or a member of your family, could win

a musical tour of Europe, all expenses paid!

1 Look at the advertisement below on your own. Which three concerts in which three cities would you/your relative most like to go to?

2 Talk to your partner and decide which three concerts you would go to together.

   1 Which concerts/places would you have to give up?

   2 How much would you have to pay if you bought the tickets yourself?

Congratulations! You have won the

competition. Now phone and book your tickets.

3 🖭 Listen to the music agent's questions. Are there still places for the concerts you want?

4 Listen again and write what the music agent says.

5 Practise the dialogue with your partner.

6 Listen to the music agent again, and answer her questions.

From *The Daily Mail*

Language review 18

1 Would (speculation)

We use *would* + main verb when we imagine, often improbable, present/future situations.

Positive

I/You/We/They	would	emigrate in that case.
She/He/(It)	('d)	

Negative

I/You/We/They	would not	emigrate in that case.
She/He/(It)	(wouldn't)	

Question

Would	I/you/we/they she/he/(it)	emigrate in that case?

Answer

Yes,	I/you/we/they/ she/he/(it)	would.
No,		wouldn't.

a Answer these questions.

What would you do if . . .

1 you saw someone breaking into your house?
2 there was a strong smell of gas in your kitchen?
3 someone came and stood in front of you in a bus queue?
4 you discovered your best friend's girl/boyfriend was having a relationship with someone else?
5 you got the bill in a restaurant but found you didn't have your wallet?
6 you were in charge of your school/work situation?

b Make five more questions like these to ask other students.

2 If + past + would (second conditional)

This expresses an improbable or impossible condition and its result.

You can use the *if* condition on its own.
Would you ever steal? *If I was* really hungry.

You can use the *if* condition with its result.
If I was really hungry, I'd steal.

c Put these words in the correct order.

1 she if would had a lot of buy she house a money
2 you met what say president if the would you
3 wouldn't abroad they choice they live had if the
4 give if a had lift I car would you a I
5 marry he you if him would asked you
6 to wouldn't didn't you we come want if ask we you

3 Make (someone) feel + adjective

Subject	+ *make*	+ pronoun	+ *feel*	+ adjective
It	makes	me/you/her/ him/it/us/ them	feel	happy. worried. angry.

·d How do these situations make you feel?

1 You see an old person sleeping rough in the street.
2 A good friend disagrees with you in a discussion about something important.
3 You hear an old school friend has died.
4 Your boss takes the credit for your idea.
5 Your parents don't like an important new friend.

4 Agree/disagree

–	+	++
I don't really agree.	I agree.	I couldn't agree more.

	I don't really agree. I didn't like it.
I think it is an excellent book.	I agree (with you). I enjoyed it.
	I couldn't agree more. It is great.

e How far do you agree with these ideas? Say something to show how you feel.

Example: Education is really important. – I couldn't agree more. The government should give more money to it.

1 Health is more important than education.
2 Taxation is too high.
3 Unemployment isn't a problem any more.
4 We are spoiling the environment for future generations.
5 Young people think about money more than they used to.

19 Do the right thing

Expressions with *say* vs *tell*

1 Preparation

1 Speak to other students. Say three things about your past life; say two true things and tell one lie.

Example: a) I was born in Timbuktu.
b) I have been married three times.
c) I bought a dress yesterday.

2 Listen to other students. What do you think? Which is their lie, a), b) or c)?

2 Vocabulary: *say* vs *tell*

1 Work with another student. Put the words below in the correct column.

Say	Tell
three things	*a lie*

three things   goodbye   a secret   a story   yes
the time   something   someone   nothing   a lie

2 Look at the expressions using *say/tell* in the questionnaire below and check your answers. Find one more word or phrase to add to each column above.

Speaking

1 Read the questionnaire below. For each situation, would you do a), b) or c)? Note your answers.

2 Ask another student and note her/his answers.

Example: A: What would you do in situation 1?
B: I'd lie.

3 Tell other students what your partner told you for each situation.

Example: She told me she'd lie about her age.

> **NB** *say* vs *tell*
>
> a) She *said* (that) she would lie about her age. ›
> b) She *told* me (that) she would lie about her age.
>
> Which sentence says who she spoke to, a) or b)?

CHOICES

1 You meet someone you like and find out s/he is much younger than you. Would you:
a) lie about your age?
b) tell the truth about your age?
c) say goodbye?

2 Your best friend tells you a secret; s/he is having an affair. Would you:
a) tell her partner?
b) tell someone else?
c) say nothing?

3 You have always disliked your bad-tempered neighbour. Now s/he is friendly and says you must come for dinner. Would you:
a) tell her/him what you thought of her/him?
b) say yes, but not go?
c) say 'No thank you' politely?

4 You are babysitting for a friend's child who won't go to sleep. Would you:
a) tell her/him another story?
b) tell her/him the time and say goodnight firmly?
c) say something else? What?

'Lady' jailed for £3 million theft

'LADY' CELIA FARRINGTON was jailed for four years after stealing nearly £3 million from the children's charity where she worked. "She spent the money on a two and a half year spending spree and an extravagant lifestyle," the court was told. The judge said four years was the lightest sentence he could possibly pass. After her trial, her lawyer told reporters she was not unhappy with the sentence. He said she would probably be out of jail within ten months.

Her fiancé, Captain Edward Parkhurst, said he was standing by

her and that they planned to get married while she was in jail. He had shared his girlfriend's extravagant lifestyle without knowing how she got the money. "I believed her story," he said. "She told us her money and title were inherited." When Ms Farrington ran away to Argentina he followed her. He then persuaded her to return and face the police.

At her trial, her lawyer said she was a lady who loved to be loved and who tried to buy friendship. In fact, Ms Farrington is unlikely to suffer too much financially. "I already have

Ms Farrington yesterday

an offer of £1 million for film rights to my story and a £500,000 offer for a book I am writing!" she told friends.

---

3 Reading

1 Look at the headline of the newspaper article above. What punishment would you give someone who stole £3 million?

2 Read the article and answer these questions.

1 Who stole the money? Who did she steal it from?

2 What sentence did she get? How long will she be in prison?

3 Is she sorry for her crime? Why/Why not?

4 What do you think? Is her punishment fair?

4 Grammar: reported statements

1 Read the article again. Who said these words: Ms Farrington/her lawyer/her fiancé/the judge?

a) 'It is the lightest sentence I can possibly pass.'

b) 'I am not unhappy with the sentence.'

c) 'She will probably be out of jail within ten months.'

d) 'I am standing by her. We plan to get married while she is in jail.'

e) 'She is a lady who loves to be loved and who tries to buy friendship.'

2 Find the reported version of these words in the newspaper article. What happens to the verbs? What happens to *I/we*?

3 Work with another student. Put these examples of direct speech into reported speech.

Ms Farrington

1 'Edward is wonderful.'

2 'I am going to buy a Caribbean island for my 30th birthday.'

Her lawyer

3 'She thinks of herself as overweight and unattractive.'

4 'We will all welcome her when she comes out.'

The judge

5 'The serious part of this matter is the large amount of money involved.'

Writing

1 Look at the examples of direct speech in the article. What punctuation shows they are the speaker's exact words?

2 Rewrite the article. Include all the new information given by Ms Farrington, her lawyer and the judge in the last exercise.

1 What is the best place for their sentences to go in the article?

2 Which new sentences will you write in reported speech/direct speech?

5 Vocabulary: large numbers

1 🖭 **Listen and write how much Ms Farrington spent.**

£ _, _ _ _, _ _ _

2 Listen again and answer these questions.

1 What words come before the commas?
2 Where do you say *and* in the number?

3 Listen and repeat the number. Then take it in turns to say these numbers to your partner.

26,790   439,301   1,303,625
87,291   957,823   5,699,123

4 Find out how Ms Farrington spent the money.

STUDENT A: Look at the chart on this page. Ask
Student B questions to complete the
missing information.

STUDENT B: Look at the chart on page 125. Ask
Student A questions to complete the
missing information.

Example: A: How much did she spend on parties?
B: £780,996.

5 Ask your partner how much she/he spends a month on the things in the chart. If you are not sure exactly, answer like this:

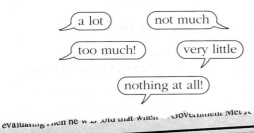

a lot
not much
too much!
very little
nothing at all!

6 Listening

1 Before you listen, answer these questions.

1 What is a radio phone-in?
2 Do you have phone-ins in your country?
3 What do people phone in about?

2 🖭 **Listen to a phone-in on British radio.**

1 Is this phone-in to a doctor, a counsellor or a
lawyer?
2 What is the caller's main problem?

3 Listen again. Which of these things did he lie about?

his nationality   his age   his address   his job
his name   his flat   his phone   his feelings

4 Check your answers with another student. Make sentences to explain his lies, like this:

He told his girlfriend his name was Pierre.

5 Talk to other students. What advice would you give Rick? Use these or other ideas to say what he should/shouldn't do.

- rent a flat in Marseilles
- take French lessons
- say he is taking English lessons and gradually
  drop the accent
- stop seeing her
- tell her parents the truth
- tell her the truth
- ask a friend to explain to her
- buy her a present
- say he has moved to London because of his job
- invite the girl on holiday to France
- run as far away as possible

6 🖭 **Listen to the end of the phone-in. Which of the advice above did the counsellor give Rick? Did you give the same advice?**

evaluating. Then he was told that when ... Government Met ...

WHERE THE CASH WENT

Parties	....
Credit Cards	£251,516
Furniture	....
Cars & Car Hire	£286,843
Flat Rent	....
Jewellery	£171,897
Spending Money	....
Staff Wages	£134,291
Travel	....
Flowers	£53,385
Wines	....
Clothes	£23,620
TOTAL £2,458,837	

he
ty
at
a
d
g
n
t
-
in
e
y
at
a
d
g
n
at
1-
n
ie
ly
at
d

7 Grammar: *If I were you*

1 📺 Listen to the counsellor's exact words and complete the sentence below.

> If I . . . you, I . . . buy a big bunch of flowers.

2 Now complete the rest of his advice.

If . . . , . . . tell her the truth.
If . . . , . . . tell any more lies.

3 Look at the completed sentences above. Is the counsellor telling Rick what he has to do or giving him advice?

Pronunciation

1 📺 Listen again and repeat the counsellor's advice, like this:

/ʷ/
If I were you, I'd buy a big bunch of flowers.

1   Is *were* stressed or unstressed in this example?
2   What does *'d* stand for?

2 Look at the situations below with another student. Take it in turns to say what your problem is. Use *If I were you . . .* to give each other advice.

Example: A: I've got a terrible headache.
B: If I were you, I'd take an aspirin.

NB *If I were/was*

a) If I *was* depressed, I'd phone.
b) If I *were* you, I'd phone.

Were is often used instead of *was* after *If*.
Which do we generally use to give advice, *was* or *were*?

8 Vocabulary: shopping rights

1 Match the expressions in column A to the definitions in column B. If you complain to a shop about faulty goods, they can:

A	B
1 give you a refund	a) do nothing
2 repair the goods	b) say sorry
3 apologise	c) give you another one
4 ignore you	d) give back money
5 give you a credit note	e) mend what you bought
6 replace the goods	f) let you buy something else in exchange later

2 Look at the situations below with two other students. What do you think? For each situation, which of the things in column A above must shops do by law in Britain?

a) You buy a pair of shoes but after two days the heel breaks.
b) You are given a hairdryer as a present. It doesn't work. The name of the shop is on the box.
c) You buy a boxed vase in a sale. A notice in the shop says 'No refunds on Sale goods'. When you unpack the vase, it is broken.
d) You buy a dress in a shop. There was no changing room so you couldn't try it on. When you get it home you don't like it.

3 Check your answers on page 126.

4 Tell other students what you think would happen in the situations above in *your* country.

ENGLISH IN ACTION

1 Read the advice below on how to complain successfully in Britain. Answer these questions with other students.

1 Which words (4 maximum) give the main idea in each section?
2 Does anything on the list surprise you?
3 Which things would/wouldn't work in your country?
4 What is the most important thing to do in your country?

Prepare to make your complaint.

2 Work in two groups. Learn part of a dialogue for complaining.

GROUP A: Look at the sentences below on this page. Each student learn one of the sentences by heart.
GROUP B: Look at the sentences on page 126. Each student learn one of the sentences by heart.

> **Group A**
> • That'll be £80 for the room and £12.50 for breakfast.
> • The parts for the Renault come to £95, plus £50 labour.
> • Can I ask you for the £10 airport tax please?
> • That'll be £30 for two set menus plus 10% for service.
> • That's £350 for the bed and £35 extra for delivery.

3 Say your sentence to students in the other group. Listen for the sentence which goes with your sentence.

4 Sit with the student who said the matching sentence and have the complete conversation.

1 Start the conversation from the beginning.
2 Include the sentence you learned.
3 Find a solution to the problem.

5 Listen to other students' conversations and answer these questions.

1 How did they solve the problem?
2 Was the conversation more successful for the customer or the person serving her/him?
3 What did she/he say to get the solution she/he wanted?

How to Complain

After talking to lawyers and the shops themselves we have put together the following ten steps to making a successful complaint.

1 Always keep receipts. It's not legally necessary but it makes complaining much easier.

2 Decide what you want before you go back. Do you want a refund, an exchange or a repair?

3 Act quickly. Go back as soon as you discover that your purchase is faulty; any delay may result in the shop claiming that you've 'accepted' the goods with the fault.

4 If you can't go in person, write. Remember, you don't have to take the goods back or to pay to return them: you can ask the shop to collect them.

5 Speak to the manager. Asking for the person in authority shows you mean business. Tell the manager exactly what's wrong with your purchase, and what you want her/him to do about it.

6 Be polite but firm. If the person you speak to refuses to help, try not to get angry. Ask for their name. If it's a chain store, also ask for the head office complaints' address.

7 If you think that you will need to complain further, it's important to keep a note of everything that has happened, and everyone you've spoken to.

8 Write to the manager. Keep it simple. Give brief details of your purchase. Say what's wrong and say what you want her/him to do. Give a time limit for action – say 14 days. Keep two copies of the letter.

9 A final letter. If you're still unhappy, write to the store manager again, but end the letter with a threat of legal action. Then send copies of all letters to the head office and ask for action.

10 If none of this has worked, seek professional advice from your local Citizens Advice Bureau.

From *Which?*

1 Verbs: *say* vs *tell*

Say	+ something	to	+ a person
He said	he was angry	to	his parents.

Tell +	person	+ something
He told	his parents	he was angry.

a Complete these sentences with *say/said* or *tell/told*.

1 He . . . he was tired.
2 We . . . them we couldn't go.
3 Please . . . Bruno I can't see him this weekend.
4 Did you . . . you loved me?
5 They didn't . . . the police.
6 You . . . me you would phone.
7 . . . thank you to Mr Jones for me.
8 The man . . . he was a detective.

2 Reported statements

In reported statements, verbs generally move one tense back.

Direct speech	Reported speech
'I *am* hungry.'	She told me/said (that) she *was* hungry.
'He *is* angry.'	She told me/said (that) he *was* angry.
'We *are* sorry.'	They told me/said (that) they *were* sorry.
'They *are talking*.'	He told me/said (that) they *were talking*.
'I *can't* go shopping.'	She told me/said (that) she *couldn't* go shopping.
'I *have* tea for breakfast.'	She told me/said (that) she *had* tea for breakfast.
'We *don't* know.'	They told me/said (that) they *didn't* know.
'I *like* the cinema.'	He told me/said (that) he *liked* the cinema.
'The doctor *will* phone.'	She told me/said (that) the doctor *would* phone.

b Report these statements. For each statement write one sentence using *say* and one using *tell*.

Example: I'm going to the cinema. – She *said* she was going to the cinema. She *told me* she was going to the cinema.

1 My husband is too tired to go out.
2 I can't take you home because I can't drive.
3 I'll help you if I can.
4 We often go to the theatre.
5 They don't know your address.
6 We are spending the weekend in France.
7 He won't come to the party.
8 I have sugar in tea but not in coffee.
9 He can come if he likes.

3 *If I were you + would* (advice)

If I were you,	I'd	phone home.
	I wouldn't	

c Give advice for the problems below. Use *If I were you . . .*

Example: A: I've got a terrible cold.
B: If I were you, I'd stay in bed.

A: It's really difficult for me to sleep at night.
B: . . .
A: My daughter comes home late every night.
B: . . .
A: I don't think I can afford to go on holiday this year.
B: . . .
A: My boss is really nasty at work.
B: . . .
A: I'm sorry I'm late. I couldn't find a parking place.
B: . . .

20 Consolidation

1 Across cultures: marriage

1 Before you read the article 'Love and marriage in Britain', complete these questions with *How much . . .* or *How many . . .*?

1 . . . couples get married in Britain every year? (About 250,000/350,000/450,000)
2 . . . prefer church to registry-office weddings? (30% /50%/70%)
3 . . . children are born illegitimate? (A third/A quarter/A half)
4 . . . marriages end in divorce? (27%/37%/47%)
5 . . . do divorces cost the country a year? (More than £0.4 million/£1.4 million/£1.4 billion)
6 . . . women depend on their husbands for money? (More than 10%/30%/50%)
7 . . . divorces each year are asked for by women? (20%/50%/70%)
8 . . . did the Prince and Princess of Wales' wedding cost in 1981? (Less than £250,000/More than £570,000/More than £1,000,000)

2 What do you think? Choose one of the answers above for each question.

3 Now read the article and check your answers.

4 Tell other students if things are the same or different in your country.

> Is the number of divorces the same in your country?

> I think so. I don't think so.

5 All these people appear at a traditional British wedding. What does each person do?

The bride —————— They help the bride.
The bridegroom ———— They are invited to the wedding.
The bridesmaids ———— He helps the bridegroom.
The best man ———— He marries the bride.
Wedding guests ———— She marries the bridegroom.

6 Write sentences about each person using *who*.

Example: The bride is the woman *who* marries the bridegroom.

7 These events describe a traditional British wedding. Number them in the order they happen.

- The bride is taken to the wedding by car. (1)
- Confetti is thrown and photographs are taken.
- Music is played so people can dance.
- Telegrams are read and toasts are made.
- The married couple's car is decorated.
- The wedding cake is cut and eaten.
- The guests are left to enjoy themselves.
- Guests are driven to the reception for a meal.
- The couple are driven away on honeymoon.
- Wedding rings are exchanged.

8 Tell other students about your own wedding or the last wedding you went to. How was it different from a traditional British wedding?

From *Options*

LOVE AND MARRIAGE IN BRITAIN

Young people in Britain may have several girlfriends or boyfriends from their teens onwards. They go to the cinema, go dancing, play sports or eat out together and do not necessarily intend to get married. However, each year about 350,000 British couples become husband and wife. Marriage is legal from the age of sixteen but most people wait until their mid to late twenties. Of those who get married, about seventy per cent prefer a traditional church wedding to a registry office wedding. However, by the age of forty, one woman in twenty and one man in eleven will still be single.

One in four children are born outside of marriage but these are not all in single-parent families; sixty per cent of unmarried parents have stable relationships. Thirty-seven per cent of marriages end in divorce and cost the country more than £1.4 billion a year. Although over thirty per cent of women depend financially on their husbands, women ask for seventy per cent of all divorces. Three out of ten divorced women married as teenagers.

Marriage does seem to be more popular now than could be imagined thirty years ago. Is it since The Prince and Princess of Wales spent over £570,000 on their Royal Wedding, since the fear of AIDS or since research has shown that married people generally live longer than the single?

2 Language in context: love

> **Revises**
> **Vocabulary**: Everyday actions
> **Grammar**: *Would* (speculation); *if* + past + *would* (second conditional)

1 Talk to other students. Think about a perfect relationship for you. What do you think?

1 Which of the things below would you want your partner to do?
2 Which would you want to do yourself?
3 If you'd prefer to share some things, who do you think would do them most often?

make sure the bills are paid   do the washing up
look after the children   mend a fuse
phone a mechanic   drive
pay in a restaurant   cook
do the shopping

2 Work with another student. Put the lines of this 1930s love song in a possible order. Think about the meaning and the rhymes.

1 . If I were the only boy in the world
. . . A garden of Eden* just made for two
. . . And I were the only boy
. . . There would be such wonderful things to do
. . . And you were the only girl
. . . Nothing else would matter in the world today
. . . I could say such wonderful things to you
. . . We would go on loving in the same old way
. . . If you were the only girl in the world
. . . With nothing to mar** our joy

> **Glossary**
> *   A garden of Eden = paradise, a perfect place
> ** to mar = to spoil, to ruin

3 📖 **Listen to the first verse of the song and check your order.**

4 What do you think? Which words would change if a woman sang the song?

5 📖 **Listen to the second verse of the song and check your answer.**

6 📖 **Listen to the last verse and sing the man or woman's part.**

Revises
Vocabulary: Selected vocabulary groups; the cinema
Grammar: *-ing* activities; *need; going to* (future)

STREET interviews

1 🔊 Listen to three people who were interviewed in the street. They were asked the question 'What do you do to improve your English outside the classroom?' What are their preferences?

A

B

C

MAKING penfriend cassettes

2 🔊 Listen. Winston is going to tell you how to make a penfriend cassette. What five things do you need?

time ____ ____ ____ ____

r a d i o MAGAZINE

3 🔊 Listen to these people phoning in for penfriends. Complete the chart then answer the questions below.

	Caller 1	Caller 2
Name		
Nationality		
Interests		
Age		

Who would you prefer to correspond with? Why?

4 🔊 Listen to Miguel Gonzalez, from Madrid in Spain. He has sent his cassette for you to hear. Which of these things does he talk about?

his family   his work   the weather   food   the radio

his studies   his school   his interests   clothes   his country

news from the BBC

5 🔊 Listen to Lisa talking about why you should listen to the news in English. She gives you two ideas to help you understand radio news more easily. What are they?

Now look at these headlines. Which countries are in the news?

6

US Elections begin

French Government says Yes!

Disaster in Japan

Economy fine - say Brazilians

British say no to high speed trains

Industrial problems in Germany

7 🔊 Listen to the radio news and answer these questions.

1 Which countries above do they mention?
2 What is the same about the three stories?

TELEVISION and films

8 📼 Listen to Winston telling you about watching television, videos and cinema films in English.

9 Look at these cinema programmes from France and Turkey. Answer the questions below.

1 What is on in English?   2 Where is it on?   3 When is it on?

No. 22-24. Sisli. Istanbul at 3 p.m.

CINEMAS

* **Readers are advised to telephone cinemas to confirm film times, since scheduled programs are sometimes changed after *Dateline* goes to press.**

Istanbul

Based on the novel by Milan Kundera, "The Unbearable Lightness of Being," directed by Philip Kaufman, starring Juliette Binoche, Daniel Day Lewis and Lena Olin, is showing at the Kadıköy Moda cinema (tel. 337-0128) at 11 a.m., 1:45, 4:30 and 9:30 p.m.; at Beyoğlu Sinepop cinema (tel. 143-7071) at noon, 3, 6, and 9 p.m. (In English with Turkish subtitles.)

"The Accused," Directed by Jonathan Kaplan, starring Jodie Foster and Kelly McGillis, is now showing at the Ortaköy Cultural Center cinema (tel. 158-6987) at noon, 2:15, 4:30, 6:45 and 9 p.m. and Kadıköy Culture and Art Center (tel. 346-0142). (In English with Turkish subtitles.)

"Ironweed," directed by Hector Babenco, starring Jack Nicholson, Meryl Streep and Carol Baker, is now showing at the Beyoğlu Emek cinema (tel. 144-8439) at 4:30 p.m. and at Kadıköy Reks cinema (tel. 336-0112) at 4:30 p.m. (In English with Turkish subtitles.)

Ankara

"Batman," directed by Tim Burton, starring Jack Nicholson, Michael Keaton and Kim Basinger, will be shown at the Akün cinema (tel. 127-7656) at 12:15, 2:30, 4:15, 7 and 9:15 p.m. (In English with Turkish subtitles.)

"Working Girl," awarded the Golden Globe, directed by Mike Nichols, starring Melanie Griffith, Harrison Ford and Sigourney Weaver, is now showing at the Kızılırmak cinema (tel. 125-5393) at 12:15, 2:30, 4:45, 7, and 9:15 p.m. (In English with Turkish subtitles.)

From *L'Officiel Des Spectacles* (vo = original version)

...05. Film 25mn après:
UNE MONDE SANS PITIE

GAUMONT CHAMPS-ELYSEES, 66, Ch. - Elysées, 43 59 04 67, Mᵉ Franklin-Roosevelt. C.B. Pl. 42 Pl. 42 F.TR 32 F: lun. + étud., CV et FN du dim. 20h au ven. 18h et – 18 ans (dim. 20h au mar.18h).
Séances: 13h50, 15h55, 18h, 20h05, 22h10.
Film 20mn après
MISS DAISY ET SON CHAUFFEUR (vo)

GEORGE V, 146, Champs-Elysées, 45 62 41 46, Mᵉ George-V. Pl. 45 F et 40 F. TR 30 F et 29 F. Lun + étud., — 18 ans et C.V. (14h á 18h30) 24F: á 12h.
1) Séances: 11h10, 13h45, 16h20, 18h55, 21h35. Film 25mn après:
IL Y A DES JOURS... ET DES LUNES (Dolby stéréo)

2) Séances: 11h30, 14h, 16h30, 19h 21h30. Film 20mn après:
LE CERCLE DES POETES DISPARUS (vo)
3) Séances: 11h55, 13h55, 15h55, 17h55, 19h55, 21h55. Film 25mn après:
LE RETOUR DE FLASH GORDON (vo)
4) GRANDE SALLE THX: Séances: 11h50, 13h50, 15h50, 17h50, 19h50, 21h50. Film 30mn après:
EINSTEIN JUNIOR (vo) (Dolby stéréo)
5) Séances: 11h45, 13h45 15h45, 17h45, 19h45 21h45. Film 25mn après:
TAPEHEADS (vo)
6) Séances: 11h30 14h, 16h30, 19h, 21h30. Film 20mn après:
NIKITA
7) Séances: 12h, 14h, 16h, 18h, 20h, 22h, Film 20mn après:
BEST OF THE BEST (vo)
8) Séances: 12h 14h, 16h, 18h, 20h, 22h. Film 20mn après:
KILL ME AGAIN (vo)
9) Séances: 11h40, 13h40, 15hh40, 17h40, 19h40, 21h40. Film 25mn après:
HAIRSPRAY (vo)
10) Séances: 11h35, 13h15, 14h55, Film 10mn après:
BLANCHE-NEIGE ET LE CHATEAU HANTE
Séances: 16h35, 19h05, 21h35. Film 25mn après:
GLORY (vo)
11) Séances: 11h50, 13h50, 15h50, 17h50, 19h50, 21h50. Film 30mn après:
FEU SUR LE CANDIDAT

From *Dateline*

GRADED readers and cassettes

10 📼 Listen to the beginning of *The 39 Steps*, and answer the questions. (The text is on page 137 if you want to read and listen at the same time.)

1 Who are the main characters?
2 What important things happen?
3 What do you think will happen next?

conclusion

11 Now make a list of the ways you plan to improve *your* English outside the classroom.

Check What You Know!

Now turn to page 130 and complete Check What You Know 4.

Communication activities

Unit 1 Exercise 7

Student B

R G Stilesmay

• A C C O U N T A N T •

279 Velasquez Court
Sheffield
South Yorkshire
S11 8XT
0742 435549

Unit 3 Exercise 4

Student A

Unit 6 Exercise 4

Student A

Unit 15 Test your memory

1 **Write the numbers in this order: 1, 3, 4, 9, 6, 10, 5, 8, 2, 7. Try to write the correct word next to each number.**

2 **Now try to improve your memory. Link the words and numbers to rhymes and images, like this:**

a) Work with another student. Choose a word to rhyme with each number from 1–10.

   Example: 1–son

b) Now look again at each word in the list on page 92. Think of a strange connection between each word and the word that rhymes with its number.

   Example: 1 (son) – newspaper – *My son* has got a newspaper on his head.

c) Now try the test again. Did you get a better score this time?

Unit 9 Exercise 5

The people thought:

1 The panel reacted mainly to my hair and mouth. This is rather unfair as my very short hair is an accident (my hairdresser's aggression not mine!) and my mouth looks unfriendly because I am very shy. Also my teeth stick out so I have stopped smiling with my mouth open! I do look a bit un-friendly but if I can stop my initial shyness then I am really sociable and friendly, not at all aggressive.

2 The panel were generally correct but some ideas were completely wrong. I'm not vain or threatening and I'm a total romantic, a lot more romantic than any woman I know. Teaching 150 students I have to be very sociable. I also love dancing and used to be sporty. The impatient bit is true: I am really impatient. I even think sleeping is a waste of time!

3 If I am objective, I also think my face is quite inviting and homely. But I am a bit more complicated than I look. True, I am very honest – it comes from a religious childhood. I'm also very shy but I can be rather aggressive. The panel saw the contradictions in my character, describing me as threatening. I'm not completely nice – who is?

From *New Woman*

Unit 11 English in Action

1 AUSTRALIAN IMMIGRATION OFFICIALS:
   Prepare to interview the applicants. Look at the immigration form below. What questions will you ask them?

2 Now interview the applicants. Your job is to:

   a) greet the applicant and introduce yourself.
   b) find out why she/he wants to emigrate.
   c) complete the form for her/him.
   d) explain that you will check references and then contact him/her again.

Prospective Immigrant: Initial interview form	az/6793

Name:_____

Marital status: single/married/widowed/divorced

Name of present spouse:_____

since:_____

Name of past spouse/s (if applicable):_____

Number of children:_____

Present address:_____

_____ since:_____

Present employment:_____ since:_____

Name and address of two referees:
1.(personal)   2.(professional)
_____   _____
_____   _____
_____   _____

Length of time known:
_____

Unit 12 English in Action

The picture is how the artist placed items in his high street to help him remember what to do before going on a skiing holiday. Going down the street on the left:

- remember to cancel the newspapers (the elephant)
- check wash bag for things like elastoplast and aspirin (on roof)
- buy film for camera
- get some foreign money in small change to use on arrival
- take out travel insurance (broken leg)
- buy books to read

On the right he continues with:

- buy new ski-goggles
- start doing ski exercises (on chimney)
- find passport
- find warm clothes

On the roundabout:

- buy suntan lotion
- decide what time to leave for the airport

Unit 13 Exercise 8

Student B

---

	week 37

Monday
11.00 swimming
5 pm visit Lisa – St Mary's Hospital

Tuesday
6.30 tennis with Malcolm

Wednesday
Doctor's 12.20 pm

Thursday
10.30 driving lesson
Lunch in town with Rachel and Alex

Friday
1.30 hairdresser's
7 pm – late Party at Joe's

Saturday
10.30 driving lesson

Sunday
4 pm meet Chris at airport

Unit 15 Would you make a good witness?

Answer these questions.

1 Where were you standing?
2 Who was standing in front of you?
3 What was the bank clerk doing?
4 What were the two men coming into the bank carrying? What did they look like?
5 What was the child doing?
6 What was the person at the counter doing? What was she wearing?

Unit 19 Exercise 5

Student B

125

Unit 3 Exercise 4

Student B

Unit 19 English in Action

Group B

But they told me airport tax was included.

But they said delivery was included.

But they told me breakfast was included.

But they said service was included.

But they told me labour was included.

Unit 19 Exercise 8

a) Under the 1979 Sale of Goods Act, you can refuse to accept faulty goods, and insist on a refund. You must do this quickly.
b) You have no right to a refund if you receive a faulty present. Only the buyer is protected by law. However, some shops will refund the money or exchange or repair the present.
c) If you buy something in the sale, and it is faulty, you can get your money back. Notices like the one in the question are illegal. However, if you buy something knowing it is not perfect, you cannot get a refund.
d) If you make a mistake when you buy something and don't like it when you get it home, the shop doesn't have to refund your money by law. However, many shops do.

Unit 17 Exercise 3

...sier ... will be to remem... er.

The man who died twice - mystery solved

1 Clive Greenwood, the man with two lives, died trying to save a friend.

5 He failed and today his wife travelled to Scotland from London to identify her husband. But she thought he had drowned ten months ago.

10 The bodies of Greenwood, 29, and 26 year-old Hilary Wells were found last Thursday in the Scottish mountains where Miss

15 Wells fell 500 feet to her death. Greenwood died of the cold as he went to get help.

As his body was formally

20 identified by his wife and his father, details of Greenwood's former life were disclosed. Before he disappeared last April, he

25 studied at King Alfred Teacher Training College. He got into trouble with the police for stealing valuable antique books but he disappeared before action could be taken.

30 Last April his yellow Volkswagen car was found near the sea with his clothes. His anxious wife

35 told the police of his disappearance and everyone believed he had drowned.

After travelling abroad,

40 Greenwood took the name Reed and went to work in Scotland. Hilary Wells started work in the same place last September. 'I

45 don't think they knew each other before she came to work here,' said their colleague Sue Bingham. She added 'He didn't talk

50 much.' The couple lived in a house nearby with Mr David Collen and his wife Jean. All four took part in regular Bible readings.

55

America raises rates

Unit 14 Exercise 1

Nikki Thomson: 35   Tom Conti: 41
Sophie Norton: 40   Alistair Blair: 33
Georgia Downs: 21   Lucille Anderson: 58

Unit 9 Exercise 1

But it's only when you get the whole picture you can fully understand what's going on.

Adapted from an original poster for *The Guardian* newspaper

Check what you know 1

1 Listening

1 🖳 Listen to a man saying how his life has changed. Put these things in the correct column.

now	before

a) in advertising
b) lots of money
c) no expense account
d) restaurant food
e) living in Spain
f) small accommodation
g) long working hours
h) an easy life
i) fresh, homegrown food
j) lots of friends
k) worse weather

2 Now write about his life. Write a sentence with *used to/didn't use to* for a)–k) above.

2 Pronunciation

Mark the stress and the number of syllables in these words.

Example: 'table (2)

accountant   creative   reporter   advertisement
interesting   independent   sunglasses   camera
photograph   museum

3 Vocabulary

Write the words which match these definitions.

a) You use this to clean your teeth.
b) The person who cuts your hair.
c) In good physical condition.
d) You put this on your body to stop the sun burning you.
e) Something you wear on your head.
f) To arrive on time for things.
g) The opposite of 'lazy'.
h) A word meaning the same as 'terrible'.

4 Grammar

Read the text below and complete each space with one word only.

I (1) . . . like living here, but there are some problems. It must be one of the (2) . . . expensive places in the world. I (3) . . . to live abroad, in Brazil. I didn't (4) . . . want to come back but in many ways I (5) . . . to because my father wasn't very well. I don't think my wife is (6) . . . unhappy about coming back as I am because she's got lots of friends here.
We (7) . . . a small flat in the suburbs a few months ago. We decided to buy a flat in town (8) . . . of a house in the country because, in the end, it makes more sense financially. I don't know how long we are (9) . . . to stay here – at least a couple of years, I think.

5 Reading

1 Read the extract from a letter below. What do you think this person's job is?

My work routine is quite hard. I have to get up around 6.30 to be sure of getting out in time for all the people coming to work in the centre of town between 7.30 and 8.30 – that's probably the busiest part of my day. A normal day finishes around 3 or 4 in the afternoon but because I need the money I often go on to 6 or 7 in the evening. I like going out to the airport because you can pick up foreign tourists and they often tip very generously (once I got a £25 tip!!).
All in all, the work's quite boring and it gets really hot in summer. The pollution on the roads is awful, you can't open your window. Really, I'm glad I'm only doing this for a short time. I'm looking forward to going back to college in October.

2 Read the letter again and write questions for these answers.

. . . ? At 6.30.
. . . ? Between 7.30 and 8.30.
. . . ? Around 3 or 4 pm.
. . . ? Because they tip well.
. . . ? No, it's quite boring.
. . . ? Because of the pollution.
. . . ? No, only a short time.
. . . ? He's going back to college.

6 Writing

Think about someone you know well. Write a description of them including:

- what they look like.
- what kind of clothes they usually wear.
- what they are like as a person.

7 Speaking

Describe a very good holiday you have had. Talk about:

- where you went.
- the food.
- the weather.
- the people.
- what you did.
- why you liked it.

Check what you know 2

1 Listening

1  Listen to a telephone conversation between two people arranging a visit to the cinema and complete this chart.

Type of Film	
Cinema	
Times	
Actors/actresses	

2 Write the questions you need to ask to get the information in the chart.

2 Pronunciation

 Listen. Which word do you hear?

1 He's very *angry/hungry*.
2 *She's sung/She sang* it lots of times.
3 Has he *run/rung* yet?
4 Is this your *cup/cap?*
5 He *ran/rang* home.
6 Where is the *hut/hat?*
7 Her *ankle/uncle* is very large.
8 What a terrible *cat/cut!*

3 Reading

Read the advertisement below and respond to two of these sentences using *must be*, two using *might be* and two using *can't be*. Justify your answers.

1 It's a routine job.
2 It's a temporary job.
3 It's really a job for a doctor.
4 It's a dangerous job.
5 The job is in England.
6 It's a demanding job.

ARE YOU INTERESTED IN AN EXCITING BUT DIFFERENT JOB?

If you are prepared to work hard, for just three months, no questions asked, for excellent pay, in a tropical climate, then apply in writing to:

**Adventure Ltd,
3, Swan Street,
Manchester, M6Q 321**

All you need is a sense of adventure, some medical experience and a lot of nerve!

4 Writing

Write a letter to find out more about the job in the advertisement. Tell them a little about:

- your education/job experience so far.
- your free time interests.
- your character.
- why you might be good for the job.

5 Vocabulary

Complete the words below, then add two more to each category.

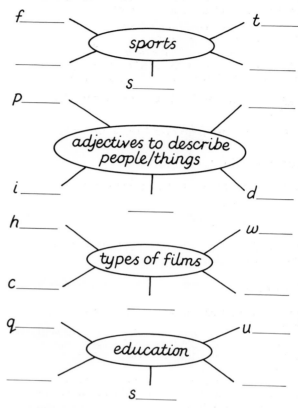

f_____   t_____
sports
s_____

p_____
adjectives to describe people/things
i_____   d_____

h_____   w_____
types of films
c_____

q_____   u_____
education
s_____

6 Grammar

Choose the correct word or phrase in each sentence.

1 What will you do *if/when* you finish your homework?
2 She is *really/quite* good at swimming but not very good.
3 I haven't opened the letter *already/yet*.
4 She *looks/looks like* beautiful, doesn't she?
5 She usually *is going/goes* to the cinema on Mondays.
6 Where *have you been/did you go* on holiday last year?
7 I *don't mind/don't like* paying for myself. In fact, I prefer it.
8 If she *will phone/phones*, I'll tell her.
9 He *could be/can't be* ill, he was fine this morning.
10 *Always/Sometimes*, she visits her mother on Sunday.

7 Speaking

Talk about what you have done in your free time recently. Have you:

- been out with friends?
- been to the cinema? What did you see? What was it like?
- played any sports? Which? Where?
- been to any interesting places? Where? What were they like?

Check what you know 3

1 Listening

1 Before you listen to an elderly couple talking about their life together, make questions to find out about them from these prompts.

1 How long/they/know each other?
2 How long/they/be married?
3 How long/they/live in/same house?
4 How long/he/work at the butcher's?
5 How long/she/have problems with her health?

2 ▣ Now listen and note the answers to your questions.

3 Write complete sentences from your notes.

2 Pronunciation

Put the words below in the correct column.

/ɒ/	/ɔː/	/əʊ/
cot	caught	coat

clock, spoke, politics, divorce, war, shop, forty, ago, water, watch

3 Grammar

Choose the correct word or phrase in each sentence.

1 I've worked here *for/since* three months.
2 He's *gone/been* to America. He gets back on Monday.
3 The soup is *too/enough* hot. I can't drink it.
4 *Although/However* we were half an hour late, the plane was still there.
5 You *don't have to/mustn't* smoke in the underground. It's against the law.
6 I *was having/had* a bath when the phone rang.
7 He *remembered/reminded* me to send my mother a birthday card.
8 What's wrong with your eye? Who *did you hit/hit you?*
9 She went to the bank *for to/to* get some money.
10 I *will phone/phone* you as soon as I know the date of the party.

4 Vocabulary

Put these letters in order to make words, then use the words to complete the sentences below.

Life changes	Shops	Political issues
ibtrh	shecmtsi	dneuiocta
rrigmaae	gnwseatsne	xtaanoit
htdae	kbrase	mupnelomtney

1 She has been very depressed since her father's . . .
2 He lost a lot of his pay rise because of high . . .
3 Get me some bread next time you go to the . . .
4 There are no jobs in the city; . . . is high.
5 I get The Times every morning at the . . .
6 They couldn't read and their general . . . was poor.

7 They are looking forward to the . . . of their fifth child.
8 We stopped at the . . . to get some aspirins.
9 . . . was disappointing. They disagreed and argued all the time.

5 Reading

Read the rules for tourists to Britain below. Complete two of these sentences with *shouldn't*, two with *don't have to* and two with *mustn't*.

1 You . . . leave your luggage unattended in public places.
2 You . . . keep your money, tickets and passport in one place.
3 You . . . drive on the right.
4 You . . . have your passport on you at all times.
5 You . . . travel without insurance.
6 You . . . buy mineral water in order to drink safely.

HOLIDAY HINTS FOR TOURISTS TO BRITAIN

DOs	DON'Ts
• Make sure hotels and restaurants welcome children before arriving with yours. • Drink the tap water. It's safe and mineral water is expensive. • Do take out adequate travel insurance. We strongly advise this as unforeseen disasters could spoil your holiday. • Remember to drive on the left!	• Leave bags and suitcases in public places unless you are with them. They could get blown up by the security forces. • Keep your money, passport and tickets in the same place, or you could lose them all. • Carry your passport around with you. You don't need it, except for changing money.

6 Writing

Write about a special occasion or your earliest childhood memory.

* What was the situation/occasion?
* Who was there?
* What were you doing/wearing/thinking at the time?
* What happened first, after that, next, finally?

7 Speaking

Talk about arrangements you have made for next week. Say:

* where you are going.
* who you are seeing.
* what you are doing.
* when you are doing each thing.

129

Check what you know 4

1 Listening

1 📠 Listen to a conversation between a father and his daughter and answer these questions.

1 What has he decided to buy for her birthday?
2 What sort does she prefer? Why?
3 What two disadvantages does her father mention?
4 What two things does she promise to do?
5 What does he suggest they do the next evening?

2 Read this summary of the conversation. Put the verbs in brackets in the correct form and put one word in each other gap.

Her father told her he (go) . . . to buy her a . . . He asked her what sort she wanted and she said she (prefer) . . . a . . . because it (be) . . . more . . . than a . . . He said he (can not) . . . afford an expensive one and she said she (not mind) . . . He reminded her that animals (be) . . . a lot of work. She said she (know) . . . and that she (will) . . . take hers for . . . and remember to . . . it. Her father said she (can) . . . meet him and choose her present the next day after work.

2 Pronunciation

📠 Listen and write the five sentences you hear.

3 Grammar

Write sentences from these prompts.

1 I/want you/give/my brother/book/tomorrow.
2 He/got/lot/money/but/not/much/time.
3 If I/be/you/I/have/holiday.
4 It/be/such/nice/day/I/go/swimming.
5 What/you do/if/not/have to/work?
6 He/tell/me/he want/go/cinema.
7 These TVs/make/Japan/and/sell/all over world.
8 He/like/people/be/interested/art.

4 Reading

Read these instructions for making an English cup of tea. Number the sentences in the correct order.

One teabag per person is put into a warm teapot. **1**

When the tea is ready, it is poured into the tea-cups.

During this time, a little milk is put into each tea-cup.

Boiling water is poured into the teapot.

Sugar is added at the end, if necessary.

The pot of tea is left to stand for about five minutes.

5 Writing

Write the instructions for making a cup of coffee, or another local drink, in your country. Make the order clear by using words like *first, then, next* and *finally.*

6 Vocabulary

Read the clues and complete the puzzle.

ACROSS
1 The opposite of *clean.* (5)
2 A machine for keeping food and drinks cold. (6)
3 We use this to wash the body. (4)
4 I need some . . . to light the fire. (7)
5 Would you prefer red or white . . . with the meal? (4)
6 Can I have a . . . of salt and vinegar crisps, please. (6)
7 A full. . . comes at the end of a sentence. (4)
8 Put all those clothes in the . . . machine. (7)
9 I'd love a small . . . of that cheese, please. (5)
10 Would you like a . . . or would you prefer to change the goods, madam? (6)

DOWN
1 A machine for cleaning plates and glasses. (10)

7 Speaking

Choose one or two of subjects 1–4 below to talk about. Say:

a) if you agree/disagree with the statement.
b) how important you think the situation is.
c) how it makes you feel.
d) what you think should happen about it.
e) what you would do if you could change things.

1 We are poisoning our planet.
2 There isn't enough discipline in modern schools.
3 The spread of English is killing other languages.
4 Unemployment is getting worse.

Tapescript

The complete tapescript can be found in the Teacher's Book.

UNIT 1

Exercise 8 Listening: 2

Conversation 1

WOMAN: Chris! Hi! I don't believe it! When did you get back?
CHRIS: Only last Wednesday. Fancy meeting you. How are you?
WOMAN: Great. What about you?
CHRIS: I'm very well.
WOMAN: Did you have a good time?
CHRIS: Yes, fantastic. Rio was wonderful.

Conversation 2

MAN: You can go in now.
JILL: Thank you.
BOB: Jill! How nice to see you! Come in, come in. Sit down. It's good to have you back in the office.
JILL: Thanks Bob. It's good to be back. How is everything?
BOB: All right, but, well, there have been a few changes while you've been away.
JILL: Oh yes, like what, for example?

Conversation 3

JIM: Hello. You must be Shu's sister.
WOMAN: That's right, and you are . . .?
JIM: I'm Jim. I'm at college with Shu.
WOMAN: Oh right.
JIM: Look, are you OK? You don't look very well.
WOMAN: I'm not too good. Actually, I feel awful. Could you get me a drink of water?

UNIT 2

Exercise 5 Listening: 3

A: She looks good, doesn't she?
B: Yeah, fantastic. She really doesn't look her age. When I think . . .
A: Here she goes.
B: No honestly, when you think what she used to look like in the sixties, she's completely different now.
A: Yes. But she was always attractive – she used to be a real hippy, flowers in her hair and everything.
B: I know but she's more beautiful and so much more confident now. She thought she was ugly then.
A: Oh she can't have!
B: Well, why change her nose otherwise? Can't you see it's straighter?
A: Yes. But it's not just her nose. She's changed her whole look. Her hair's curlier now. I also heard she had bits taken out of her legs. They're certainly thinner.
B: Oh no! That must hurt. I couldn't . . .
A: And look at her face. It's still so attractive. She's definitely had a face-lift. And you must admit, she does look better.
B: Yes, but it's not right is it? Do you know how much all that costs?
A: A fortune! It's terrible really.
B: I think it's awful. But . . .
A: What?
B: I do hate my ears. I'd love to do something.
A: Oh no! Not really! You're mad. Your ears are fine. You look great! Fantastic. Don't be stupid! You don't really mean it.
B: No, I don't. I think cosmetic surgery is awful, a disgrace, terrible . . . haven't got enough money anyway.

UNIT 3

Exercise 2 Listening: 1

C: Martine, you are lucky, you know, going to Paris for the weekend. I wish I was coming with you.
M: Me too. Trouble is, I've got to work.
C: Yeah, but you enjoy your work. Anyway, it's better than going to Philip's for dinner.
M: Oh, I wanted to go.
C: Well, I don't. In fact, I don't know why I'm going.
M: Well, I'll think about you when I'm in my nice, comfortable first-class hotel . . .
C: Yeah, you do that. Look, you'd better hurry. You're going to miss

the plane if you're not careful. Which of these things on the bed do you need?
M: I'll take my sunglasses, my walkman and the map.
C: What do you need a map for?
M: To get to the conference hall from the hotel.
C: Oh right. Well, what else do you need? What about the camera?
M: No, I don't think so. No time to take photographs.
C: What, no time at all?
M: No, it's a meeting. I'm not going to be a tourist. Pass me my passport and traveller's cheques, will you? They're over there on the table.
C: OK. Here you are.
M: Now, where's my briefcase? I need those papers for the meeting.
C: Here it is. There's the taxi. Come on, let's go. Now, are you sure you don't want to take your camera?

UNIT 4

Exercise 8 Listening: 2

M: Ah, there you are, Jim. Late again.
J: I'm sorry, but . . .
M: Well sorry's no good, is it? This is the third time in three weeks. The company doesn't exist for you, you know. Everyone else gets here on time. Look! All here, working away. Doing your work, as well as theirs. It's not fair, is it?
J: No, but . . .
M: No, it's not fair. What have you got to say for yourself?
J: Nothing.
M: Nothing. Well, if you come in late again, you won't have to come back. We don't want people who can't be punctual.

Exercise 8 Listening: 3

M: Ah, Jim, there you are.
J: I'm sorry but . . . I can't manage . . .
M: Now, what's the trouble?
J: I'll go and start work.
M: No. I want to know why you are late.
J: I'm tired.
M: Yes?
J: Well, I live with my old mum and I look after her without any help but the week before last she had a bad fall, (Oh dear) she fell down the stairs. She's eighty-one you know and she can't be left alone. I've got someone to come and look after her every morning at eight o'clock but sometimes she's late and I have to wait for her.
M: Yes. I see. Well, you organise things at home, so if you have to be late a few mornings, that's OK, we'll cover for you.

UNIT 5

Exercise 3 Language in context: 2

A: I really enjoyed seeing Paula last week, didn't you?
B: Yes, she seems to love her work.
A: Yes, it's great. She used to have problems with her boss, you know.
B: I know but things are better now and she . . .
C: Excuse me. Are you ready, or would you like a few more minutes?
A: No, I think we're ready, aren't we, Paul?
B: Yes, I think so.
C: Fine. Now, what would you like?
A: Oh dear. I can't remember what I de . . . Oh yes, I'll have the minestrone soup to start with and then . . . what's today's special?
C: Um, it's Spaghetti Carbonara.
A: What is that, exactly?
C: It's spaghetti with bacon in a cream sauce.
A: Hm. That sounds nice. I'll have that. And a green salad please.
C: Right. And what would you like, Sir?
B: I'll have the soup too, please. And then the Lasagne.
C: Fine. Now, what would you like to drink?
A: A bottle of house red, please, and can we have some. . .

UNIT 6

English in action: 2

Well, it became a serious hobby about six years ago. I went skiing with my family in the Alps and found I preferred watching and painting to going on the ski-slopes. I'd always enjoyed art at school but after that holiday it became a passion. I spend my time on holidays now visiting art galleries and collecting postcards of pictures I particularly like. I paint seriously at the weekends but I usually draw or sketch something every day. I particularly like drawing people and landscapes – the countryside – using watercolours and oil paints. This means I can be sociable and go out with my friends. For example, one of my friends goes fishing a lot and I go with him. He fishes and I paint. That's one of the things I like about this hobby – you can do it indoors and outdoors so I can take advantage of the good weather too. I take private lessons once a week with a really good teacher. It's expensive but I don't mind spending money on this – I enjoy it so much.

UNIT 7

Exercise 3 Listening: 1

1 It was very frightening. I love horror movies. I think they're great!
2 It was disgusting. All that sex and violence. Films like that shouldn't be allowed!
3 It wasn't very good, a bit long and boring really. I wouldn't want to see it again. It was disappointing. I thought it would be better.
4 It was good. The beginning was exciting. Other people's problems are always interesting even if they are a bit depressing.
5 It was all right, quite an amusing film. Not fantastic but not bad.

UNIT 8

Exercise 7 Listening: 1

I: So, tell me a little about the different schools you've been to.
S: Well, I've always been to state schools ever since I started school. My parents never had a lot of money. Apparently they would like to have sent me to a private school but they couldn't afford it.
I: What did you think of your very first school?
S: I loved my primary school, our teachers were wonderful. We had a great time but we learnt a lot as well. I was very sad to leave it when I was 10.
I: I know, it's hard isn't it?
S: Yes, but I soon settled in to my new school. I didn't like the teachers so much but I made one or two good friends which meant it wasn't too bad. I've been at this school for nearly seven years now.
I: Really? And what about exams? What exams have you taken?
S: Um . . . I took GCSEs in Maths, English, French, Science, and, um, Geography, Art and Religious Education when I was 16 and then I had to choose 3 subjects to study for A levels for the next 2 years. Those are the only really important exams, GCSEs and A levels. Anyway, I decided to do Maths, Physics and Chemistry for A level. It's been hard work but I've enjoyed it. My exams are in June.
I: Right. Um, what then?
S: Well, If I pass my A levels I'll go to university. Which university I go to will depend on the grades. If I fail I don't know what I'll do. I suppose I'll have to retake them or maybe I'll just start looking for a job. Anyway, in July I'm going to hitchhike around Europe with my boyfriend for a couple of months. I'm really looking forward to it.
I: I'm not surprised. It sounds great.

UNIT 9

Exercise 8 Listening: 2
Chorus
It must be love I'm feeling
This must be love
This must be love I'm feeling
This must be love

Verse 1
Well, I wait in every day
Oh just in case you decide to call
And I can hardly wait
'Cos I never thought time could pass so slowly

(Chorus)

Verse 2
Happiness is something I never thought I'd feel again
And now I know
Oh, it's you that I've been looking for
And day by day, more and more

Verse 3
Well, I know what you think
You've heard it before
Don't tell me I know
That this feeling inside my heart
Well, you know, never letting go, cos I've been there

(Chorus)

Verse 4
Words can only say so much
It's hard to express
Oh, the things you do to me
You're everything I could ever dream you would be

(Chorus)

Exercise 8 Listening: 4
PHIL: Oh, where haven't I been would probably be quicker. Actually, there's an awful lot of ground that we haven't travelled. We've never been to Russia, for instance, never been to China, Africa. So, there's been lots of large expanses of area we've never, never, sort of, managed to get to.
INT: Have you been to Japan?
PHIL: Oh yeah. Japan we've been to 3 or 4 times and it's a very interesting place to play. I mean I love the food there anyway, Japanese food's one of my favourite foods. And, um, it's so different that it's so interesting.
INT: How do the audiences differ say in Latin America to Japan?
PHIL: Well, in Japan they all sing along to the records, they all sing along to the songs when you're singing them in concert but they don't really understand what they're singing I don't think. Um, some of them do I suppose because they've, they're taught English and some of them speak very good English considering it's culture you know, completely different sort of culture. Um. They're very rowdy in South America, in Latin countries, I mean, that's including places like Spain and what have you. Er, each country's got its own type of reaction, um. But we've played in so many different places and we've all got a soft spot for lots of them: Italy is always great to play, um most of the European countries now are really good. Germany was a bit of a problem for us in the early days but it's strong for us now so . . . they've all got their own little identity to be quite honest.

English in action: 8
WOMAN: Excuse me.
MAN: Yes?
WOMAN: I'm trying to find a particular song. Can you help me?
MAN: Well, I can try.
WOMAN: Have you got 'Angel' by The Eurythmics?
MAN: The Eurythmics? Which album is it on? Do you know?
WOMAN: No, sorry, I don't.
MAN: Well, let me see. Oh yes, here it is. It's on 'We Too Are One'. I think we've got that. Do you want CD, tape or record?
WOMAN: CD, I think.
MAN: Right. They're over there on the right. The album's called 'We Too Are One' under E for Eurythmics.
WOMAN: Great, thanks.
MAN: That's OK.

UNIT 10

Exercise 1 Across cultures: 2
SUE: You seemed really surprised in that restaurant the other night. Do you think I left too big a tip?
BETH: No, I thought you left too little.
SUE: Too little?
BETH: Yes.
SUE: But I left ten percent.
BETH: Yeah, but Americans tip fifteen and that's what I'm used to.
SUE: Fifteen?
BETH: Yeah.
SUE: Oh, that seems a lot. You don't do that in England do you?
BETH: I try not to but it's difficult.
SUE: Goodness! What about when you go out with men in the States? Who pays?
BETH: Usually the man, if, if he invites me to go out then I expect him to pay.
SUE: Really, even if he's another student?
BETH: Yeah, if I want to pay we can talk about it and usually there's no problem.
SUE: Right, but you must talk about it before you offer your part.
BETH: Absolutely.
SUE: Oh, that's strange.
BETH: It needs to be clear.
SUE: I think in Britain probably if you're students you pay half and half, er, not all couples but students I think. Yeah, yeah, that's really quite different. Um, if for example I borrowed some money from you say, something very little, to buy a packet of cigarettes for example and I didn't give you the money back the next day, how would you feel about that?

BETH: Um, a bit anxious. I would expect you to pay me back.
SUE: But I'm a friend Beth!
BETH: Well I know, and I know that you'd pay me back but I would expect you to pay me back even for a packet of cigarettes.
SUE: Yeah, I think the British are like that too. Let me ask you another thing. If you found ten dollars in the street.
BETH: Uh huh.
SUE: Only ten dollars right. If money's important would you take it to the police station?
BETH: Not ten dollars, no.
SUE: Ah you see. So what would you do?
BETH: I'd keep it. If I found a lot of money I'd take it to the police but not ten dollars.
SUE: No, I think it's the same here.

Exercise 3 Thinking about learning: 2

1
A: Liz, what language have you learnt?
B: Um, I've just finished doing a course in Russian.
A: Russian! That sounds really exciting. Where did you learn it?
B: That was, er, that was a course of evening classes at a local college here.
A: And how many evenings did you go?
B: Um. Just one evening a week, we went for two hours every week, which wasn't really enough, I don't think.
A: You'd need to go more often to make it worthwhile?
B: I think so, if you were going to learn the language properly, yes.
A: Mm. How did they teach it?
B: Um. It was quite a traditional method really. We did a lot of grammar exercises, um, obviously the grammar's quite different, quite important in Russian. Um. That was OK. I didn't mind that. I actually quite like grammar.
A: Any other techniques?
B: Um. Yeah, there was, er, a video course.
A: What did that involve?
B: That was, it went with the book that we were using and, er, we used to watch a one hour video each week of people talking Russian, real Russians, um, so that was good, that was an interesting way to learn.
A: You really enjoyed that?
B: Yeah. I think it was a more valid way to learn, really.
A: Was there a part of the course then that wasn't very satisfactory?
B: Yeah, we did a lot of translation in class, really again it was the traditional approach, um, reading around the class, taking turns to translate things around the class, which, basically was too difficult, um, for our level, we couldn't do it at all really.
A: Mm. So if, um, you know, if someone else was going to study at an evening class would you recommend it as a way of learning?
B: I think it depends on the course, um, and the teacher obviously. I don't think I'll be going back to that particular college next year.

2
A: Steve, what language have you learnt?
B: German.
A: German? And how did you learn it?
B: Self-taught.
A: You taught yourself. Now, what does that involve?
B: Well, in my case that involved using phrase books, dictionaries, and parallel texts.
A: Parallel texts? What are they?
B: Well, parallel texts are when you have a story and the story is in two languages, in this case of course, German and English. And you would have the German on one side of the page and the English on the other side of the page. Um, I used to, understandably, I used to buy stories I liked, and stories in fact that I'd already read in English and so then I could read the German, remembering what I'd read in English.
A: So, um, you really enjoyed that way of learning really?
B: Very much.
A: Yeah. And, OK, you were learning from dictionaries and and parallel texts and phrase books, but when you were in conversation with people, did you find any difficulties at all?
B: Um, I often found difficulties, um, but I had a number of friends who used to correct me, um, and that was in fact very helpful, I didn't mind being corrected.
A: That was OK?
B: That was a great assistance, yes.
A: Mm. And so, I mean I suppose if you're teaching yourself, um, there must be a lot of motivation about it all – are there any negative things at all, anything you didn't enjoy doing?

B: Certainly, certainly, yes. I didn't like studying the grammar by myself and, I think as a result of that, my German isn't as good as I would like it to be.

3
A: Janet, do you speak a foreign language?
B: Mm, yes, yes I do. I'm fluent in Spanish.
A: Really? How did you learn it?
B: Well, I went and lived in Spain for, er, two years. Um, I lived in Madrid.
A: Sounds great.
B: Mm, it was
A: Did you know people there?
B: Yes, I had, some friends out there, um, which was great when I first arrived, to know some people there.
A: How did you go about learning the language, um, you know, did you just talk to people or were there other ways?
B: No, lots of ways. Um, I used to watch television. Um, I'd watch the news in Spanish for example and try to work out what was going on, um and of course I watched lots of other programmes, that was very useful, watching television.
A: What other ways?
B: I also used to buy cassettes of, um, pop songs, you know, modern pop songs and, um, I'd learn the words and sing along in Spanish to the words.
A: And which of those did you really like doing?
B: I loved the songs. That was great, and I learnt a lot.
A: Right.
B: But, um, another thing I did which, um, which was useful, but not so much fun as singing songs, was, um, I used to write lists of vocabulary, you know, long lists of words, yeah, it was hard work but, um, I didn't mind that because it was so useful. I learnt a lot.
A: I suppose if you were going out there and learning it the way you, you know, really wanted to, there wasn't a lot that you perhaps wouldn't enjoy, but is there something that really, you know, was the most boring thing?
B: Oh, what I didn't like, the worst thing, um, was being corrected by my friends, you know, you're sitting in a bar or café and, um, and everything you say they're correcting. I didn't like that.
A: Right.
B: But over all, I mean, going to the country, going to Spain to learn Spanish was wonderful. I'd recommend anybody to do it.
A: Yeah.

Images
See Additional Tapescripts at the end of the Teacher's Book.

UNIT 11

Exercise 1 Preparation: 2

Where have all the flowers gone?
Where have all the flowers gone, long time passing?
Where have all the flowers gone, long time ago?
Where have all the flowers gone?
Young girls have picked them every one!
When will they ever learn? When will they ever learn?

Where have all the young girls gone, long time passing?
Where have all the young girls gone, long time ago?
Where have all the young girls gone?
Gone for husbands every one!
When will they ever learn, when will they ever learn?

Where have all the husbands gone, long time passing?
Where have all the husbands gone, long time ago?
Where have all the husbands gone?
Gone for soldiers, every one!
When will they ever learn, when will they ever learn?

And where have all the soldiers gone, long time passing?
Where have all the soldiers gone, long time ago?
Where have all the soldiers gone?
Gone to graveyards, every one!
When will they ever learn, when will they ever learn?

And where have all the graveyards gone, long time passing?
Where have all the graveyards gone, long time ago?
Where have all the graveyards gone?
Gone to flowers, every one!
When will they ever learn, when will they ever learn?

Repeat first verse.

Exercise 7 Speaking: Grammar: 4

1
A: Margaret, what's your most treasured possession?
B: Um, I think, I think it's probably a pen.
A: A pen? What kind of a pen?
B: That's, er, it's a rather nice old-fashioned kind of fountain pen, one of the ones that you have to put the ink in yourself.
A: And who gave you that?
B: That was my mum.
A: Your mother gave it to you?
B: Yeah.
A: That's nice. When did she give it to you?
B: Well, let's think. It would be about seven years ago now, I suppose, while I was at university.
A: And why did she give it to you?
B: It was a time I was doing my final exams and I was feeling a bit uncertain about them, I wasn't sure if I was going to pass or not so she gave me the pen as a sort of a good luck charm.
A: And that's really why it's so special to you, because it's a lucky charm.
B: Uh huh. Yeah, and it actually worked because I did pass the exams in the end and it's also a very nice pen.

2
A: Richard, what's your most treasured possession?
B: I think, probably it would be my Pentax camera, actually, yeah.
A: Was it a present?
B: Yes it was. Um. My grandfather gave it to me, er, a while ago now, in fact.
A: How long ago?
B: That must be ten years ago, I think, yeah.
A: Why did he give it to you?
B: It was just before I got my first job abroad. It was in Cairo, in Egypt and, er, he gave it to me because I was leaving.
A: And why is it so special to you?
B: I think it is really special because I've been travelling, um, quite a bit in the last few years and it's always gone with me everywhere I've been and it's, er, with it I've been able to take lots of photographs and they're memories for me so it's really been the source of a lot of special memories.

3
A: Susannah, what's your most treasured possession?
B: Um, I think it's my car.
A: Was it a present?
B: No, I bought it myself, but I had to save a lot of money for it first.
A: Right, and so you're very fond of it?
B: Yes, I am. It was, it was quite cheap and nothing special but it's got a lot of character.
A: When did you buy it?
B: Um, I bought it about a year ago, so it still feels quite new and exciting.
A: So what makes it so special for you?
B: Um, well it gives me my independence. I don't have to rely on my friends to drive me to places. I can go wherever I like. I like travelling, um, and so I can take it on holiday with me.

UNIT 12

Exercise 3 Listening: 2

1
I remember exactly what I was doing when I heard Marlene Dietrich had died. I was at the theatre in London. I went to see *The Phantom of the Opera*. We heard the news in the interval. I was buying an ice cream at the time. It made me feel rather old.

2
When I heard there had been another big earthquake in San Francisco, I was playing tennis with my father. We were on vacation and my mother came running to tell us the news. Our house had been completely destroyed. There was nothing left.

3
There were a lot of changes in many countries at the time but I really didn't think it could happen in Germany so quickly. I couldn't believe it when I heard people were knocking the wall down. I turned off the radio and phoned my German friend Birgit to tell her.

4
I wasn't really surprised. We were expecting Mandela's release from prison, but when my friend told me I was so pleased for a minute I couldn't do anything. I was shaving, in fact, which was a shame because I stopped dead and cut myself.

UNIT 13

Exercise 6 Listening: 1

I: Mr Blair, what party are you in?
TB: I'm in the Labour Party. I joined the Labour Party when I was aged about 20 years old and it's the only political party that I have joined and I came into Parliament for the Labour Party in 1983, so I've been in Parliament now for some considerable period of time.
I: Of these key political issues here, which do you think are the most important ones now?
TB: The economy is always of enormous importance. There have been great problems with, er, British industry and the fact that we have been importing very many more goods than we've actually been exporting abroad, and so it's important to build up our economy and build for future economic success. Unemployment is immensely important, particularly amongst young people because we have had large numbers of young people unemployed for long periods of time and the issues, I think, of the future, are going to be issues such as the environment and childcare because whilst the issues of the economy and to some extent, unemployment, are always going to be with us, I think the issues of the future revolve around the question of how women can both work and bring up a family which is the issue of childcare and the environment which I think is of much greater importance today than it has been traditionally.

Exercise 6 Listening: 2

I: You must have a very full diary, can you tell me what you're doing next week?
TB: On Monday I start at 10 o'clock in the morning with a speech to a conference in London about crime and the problems of crime particularly, um, in the London area. Later in the day, round about 4 o'clock in the afternoon, the government will publish its new proposals on immigration and I will be responding to those on behalf of the Labour Party. And then in the evening, round about 7 o'clock, I will be taking some constituents of mine from the north of England round a tour of Parliament.
I: On to Tuesday.
TB: On Tuesday I will be going out to the constituency, and I will be having lunch first of all, at round about 1 o'clock with the Chamber of Commerce in my constituency that looks after business interests there and I will also be opening a new road to the airport in my constituency which is something we have been asking for for a long time. And then in the evening I will be presenting awards at a local community college to those that have undergone education and training within our area.
I: What time will that be?
TB: That will be round about 8.30 but then there will be a social function after that, a dinner, and we will be eating with some of the students and so there will be a chance to talk with them too. And indeed I think also that day I'm fitting in a recording of a television programme about the coal industry as well, so I will be having a fairly busy time. I think that's round about 6 o'clock in the evening.
I: OK. Then on to Wednesday.
TB: On Wednesday, I will be holding surgeries in my constituency, that is where my constituents will come to me with particular problems that they have, problems say with housing, or with, um, difficulties in finding work, and I will see them, and then later that day there is, er, what is called an open day at a local factory which means that the factory invites people to come in and see what is happening in the factory, see the products of the factory and those that work there will take part in that.
I: That's at what time?
TB: And that will be round about 2 o'clock in the afternoon.
I: Right, let's move to Thursday, then.
TB: On Thursday, I'm having a meeting with the fire brigade in the London area because there have been a lot of difficulties in the London area recently with fires and in particular with the additional funding that is required, the money that is needed by the fire brigade to carry out their duties in London. And then I will also be having a meeting a little bit later, round about 12 o'clock, er, that morning, with those that are concerned with the reform of our prison system in Britain because we have had a very serious problem with overcrowding, with too many people in the prisons and I will be meeting those who are campaigning for changes in the prison system, and then later that day, at 4 o'clock, I will be meeting with the heads of various department stores to talk about whether Britain should allow trading in shops, shops to be open on Sundays.
I: And finally Friday?

UNIT 14

Exercise 5 Grammar: Listening: 1

SUE: But surely you agree that young people in America have more freedom, can do more what they want than in Britain?

BETH: Well, yes but it varies from state to state.

SUE: Are there different laws from state to state?

BETH: There are very different laws and for example I come from Salt Lake City in Utah.

SUE: Oh, yeah! You're not from San Francisco.

BETH: No. No. Seventy-five percent of the people in Utah are Mormon and Mormon laws very much affect our lives.

STEVE: Gosh.

SUE: Right, OK so they are sort of religious laws?

BETH: Well they're religiously based laws, no, they're not religious laws per se.

SUE: Uh huh, and what, give me some examples of things you can or can't do.

BETH: Well for example we really shouldn't smoke or drink alchohol.

SUE: Not at all?

BETH: Not at all and, for example, my parents don't drink tea or coffee.

STEVE: But then you drink tea or coffee then?

BETH: Well the odd cup. Just the odd cup.

SUE: I'm surprised you can eat meat.

BETH: Well, Joseph Smith the founder of the Mormon church recommended against it. He said that it would be better to eat lots of fresh fruit and vegetables but now everything's in moderation and so we eat some meat.

SUE: Right, and is it true that men can have more than one wife?

BETH: No, it's not true any longer.

SUE: Oh really!

BETH: It was only in the past that they could have more than wife.

STEVE: Uh huh, how many could they have?

BETH: I think up to four.

SUE: Really. And can Mormons marry non-Mormons?

BETH: They can but, for example, if I married a non-Mormon my marriage would only be for life, not for eternity.

SUE: Oh really. And what age can you get married?

BETH: As early as fourteen.

STEVE: I see, and that's the same for boys and girls?

BETH: It is the same yeah. It's a bit early in Utah.

SUE: Yes it is – fourteen goodness! And that's if the parents agree?

BETH: That is if the parents agree, yes. If the parents don't agree then kids have to wait until they're eighteen.

SUE: Right, OK, and when can they leave school?

BETH: Sixteen.

SUE: That's the same here.

BETH: Yes, it's the same everywhere in the States, that's the federal minimum age.

SUE: Right, OK, and then I suppose the boys go in the army?

BETH: No, there's no military service in the States.

SUE: Oh!

STEVE: But there was wasn't there, a few years ago?

BETH: There was, there was a draft during the Vietnam war but not any more.

SUE: But not now.

BETH: Uh uh.

SUE: So they don't go in the army at all?

BETH: No, not at all.

UNIT 15

Exercise 1 Across cultures: 2

1

A: Hello Tessa. How old are you?

B: Nine years old.

A: And where do you live?

B: London.

A: Whereabouts in London?

B: North London.

A: And, er, have you always lived in London?

B: No, we lived three years in Spain.

A: Really? Why was that?

B: Because I was born in Spain and my, and my grandparents are from Spain.

A: You're grandparents are, and what about your mum and dad?

B: My mum's Spanish and my dad's English.

A: Oh right, so do, you know, do you think you're English or Spanish?

B: Half English, half Spanish.

A: So, um when you're at home, is there anything you have to do?

B: Um, go to bed at the right time.

A: I see. What time?

B: Half past nine.

A: Uh huh. And how about helping around the house - do you have to do any housework?

B: Not normally.

A: Right. Now is there anything that you mustn't do?

B: Speak English to my mum.

A: I see. So, er, you know, when you compare parents in England and parents in Spain, do you think, er, your parents are particularly strict?

B: Not really.

2

A: Hi, Manuel. How old are you?

B: I am 15

A: And, er, where do you come from?

B: I come from Peru.

A: Whereabouts in Peru?

B: Lima.

A: That's the capital city?

B: Yes.

A: And, um, where do you live now?

B: Now I live in London.

A: Why is that?

B: Well, my parents are both working here.

A: They're both Peruvian, of course.

B: Yes.

A: And, um, how do your parents compare with English parents - are they, er, stricter or less strict?

B: They're stricter.

A: Now, why do you say that, in what way are they stricter?

B: Well, er, when I'm out they're always asking who I'm going to be with and where I'm going to be.

A: Talking about your parents and home, um, what do you have to do at home?

B: Er, tidy my room, keep it clean and do the dishes.

A: You do that every day?

B: Er, no, I take it in turns with my mother and father.

A: Right. Um, do you have to do things like visiting your grandparents, go and see them back in Peru?

B: Er, no, but I like to.

A: How often?

B: Every 2 years.

A: And, um, is there anything you mustn't do?

B: Well, let the dog into the house.

A: What kind of dog have you got?

B: It's an Alsatian.

A: And you mustn't let it in the house at all?

B: No.

A: Really. Where does it live?

B: It lives outside, in a kennel.

3

A: Hi, Sarah. How old are you?

B: I'm sixteen.

A: And where do you live?

B: I live in Paris.

A: Wow, that's very nice. Why are you in England then?

B: Well, I come to England to see my dad.

A: Uh huh. And who do you live with in Paris?

B: I live with my mum in Paris.

A: Right. Is she French?

B: Yeah. My mum's French and my dad's English.

A: Right. So how do you see yourself then - English, French, or what?

B: I think I see myself as more English, really.

A: Why is that?

B: Um. I spent most of my younger life in England, and I feel that I can relate to English people more than French people.

A: Mm. Is your mum very strict?

B: Um. Yeah, I'd say she was fairly strict.

A: How is she strict?

B: Um. She's very strict about work, school work.

A: Oh, I see. And, er, how does she compare with your dad?

B: Well, I don't live with my dad so it's not the same, but I'd say she was more strict than my dad.

A: Um. When you're in your mum's house, is there anything you have to do?

B: I have to do my homework before I go out.

A: Right. And anything you mustn't do?

B: I mustn't go out late without phoning her first, tell her where I am.
A: How about pocket money? Do you get pocket money in France?
B: Yeah, I do.
A: Do you have to buy everything with that?
B: I have to pay for most things but I don't have to buy my own clothes, my mother buys them for me.
A: I see. So, where would you rather be, in Paris or in England?
B: I'd rather be in England I think.
A: Why?
B: Um. I think I like the lifestyle more in England, and I have a few more friends in England.

UNIT 16

Exercise 5 Listening: 1

I know an old lady who swallowed a fly
I know an old lady who swallowed a fly.
I don't know why she swallowed the fly.
Perhaps she'll die.

I know an old lady who swallowed a spider,
that wriggled and tickled and tickled inside her.
She swallowed the spider to catch the fly.
I don't know why she swallowed the fly.
Perhaps she'll die.

I know an old lady who swallowed a bird.
How absurd! She swallowed a bird.
She swallowed the bird to catch the spider, etc.

I know an old lady who swallowed a cat.
Fancy that! She swallowed a cat .
She swallowed the cat to catch the bird, etc.

I know an old lady who swallowed a dog.
What a hog! She swallowed a dog.
She swallowed the dog to catch the cat, etc.

I know an old lady who swallowed a goat.
She opened her throat and swallowed a goat.
She swallowed the goat to catch the dog, etc.

I know an old lady who swallowed a cow.
I don't know how she swallowed the cow!
She swallowed the cow to catch the goat, etc.

I know an old lady who swallowed a horse.
She's dead, of course!

Exercise 7 Vocabulary: Pronunciation: 4
See Additional Tapescripts at the end of the Teacher's Book.

Exercise 9 Reading: Listening: 1
Yeah, it's true. I love chocolate. I suppose I am addicted to it. I always carry a couple of bars around with me. I hate to think I can't have some when I want some. I don't know how much I eat a week, but I know I spend about £150 on it a month. I know that because it's caused money problems at home and I've had to borrow money from my parents to pay some of the bills.
I usually have a black coffee and a Mars bar or two for breakfast. I can't eat anything else – the thought of cereal or toast makes me feel quite sick. I think I eat more chocolate when I feel depressed and also when I have a lot of work to do, it keeps me going. My husband doesn't like the way I eat so much – he says it's unhealthy but then he smokes and I don't like that, so he can't really say anything, can he? And anyway I never have any problems with my teeth and I don't get fat, so I don't see why I should stop.

English in action: 6
BANK CLERK: Hello. Good morning. What can I do for you?
WOMAN: Hello. I'd like to cash this cheque, please
BANK CLERK: Fine. No problem. How would you like it, in 10s or 20s?
WOMAN: Oh, um, in tens, please. I'd also like to send some money to the States, if that's possible.
BANK CLERK: To America?
WOMAN: Yes, I've got the account number.
BANK CLERK: Ah, well, you need the overseas counter. That's not me, I'm afraid. You'll need that queue over there.
WOMAN: Oh. OK. Just one more thing.
BANK CLERK: Yes?
WOMAN: How do I apply for some sort of credit card. I haven't got one and I thought I . . .
BANK CLERK: Oh that's simple. Just fill in this form and send it in.

WOMAN: Oh, I can't get one immediately, then? Oh, I hoped. . .
BANK CLERK: I'm afraid not. It has to be sent in.
WOMAN: OK. I'll do that then. Thanks for your help.
BANK CLERK: Not at all. Goodbye.

UNIT 17

Exercise 6 Listening: 1
1
My heroine is Indira Ghandi. She was really strong. India was a big and divided country. She kept it together – united. She travelled a lot and she was cosmopolitan in attitude, open to other countries. She understood other nationalities and represented India well to the rest of the world. She valued the traditions of her country too so she didn't make too many changes too quickly. Some people say she was cruel but I think she was strong. She was a woman in a man's world. People respected her – she was such a respected person. That's such an important thing for a politician.

2
I think Martin Luther King is the person I admire most. He dreamed of a better, less racist world. Although he faced violence throughout his life he didn't change his ideas. He didn't use violence but, er, he did fight the system. He was such a gentle, non-violent man. He led a quarter of a million people in Washington demanding that black people be given the vote. Thanks to him, black people were given the vote in 1962. He was so sure he was right. I would love to be that certain of things.

3
My favourite person is Marilyn Monroe. I know she isn't really a historical person but she represents something important to me. She was such an ordinary person with such big dreams. I think everyone needs dreams. She had such an unhappy life but, even so, she tried hard to enjoy it. She was so beautiful and successful on one level but so frightened and alone on another. That's why I like her I think. Her life was a disaster although she was in such a lot of successful films. She represents success and disaster – a good warning for life!

UNIT 18

Exercise 6 Listening: 1
1
I: This week our castaway is the actor Anthony Hopkins. Tony, I know that music means a great deal in your life, you play the piano?
AH: Yes.
I: Were you put to it or did you take to it?
AH: I took to it quite early, I started at about the age of six.
I: Did you ever consider taking it up professionally?
AH: Yes, I did for a while, er, for about ten years I think and then I discovered that I didn't have the technique or the talent really to play as a concert pianist. That's what I wanted to be, was a concert pianist so I more or less gave up, or it gave me up.
I: Yes, the top or nothing.
AH: Top or nothing, that's been it all my life, yes.
i: Do you play discs a lot?
AH: Yes, I play music a lot when I'm working on plays, you know, I choose something that will help me get in the mood when I'm reading.
I: Well you have just eight for what may be a long time. How did you set about choosing them. Are you choosing nostalgically?
AH: They're nostalgically, yes I've chosen a few that, um, made an impression on me when I was a child.

2
I: Did you pick up enough local knowledge to put up a hut, do you think, some kind of shelter?
AH: No, I can't even knock a nail in a wall.
I: Well, you wouldn't have any nails.
AH: No, I wouldn't have any nails. All I would want to take is a piano. Of course I can't take a piano with me.
I: Yes you can that's your luxury.
AH: A piano tuner?
I: Not a tuner, no.
AH: Well I'll take a piano and tune it myself.
I: Right. What about food. Any idea? Can you fish?
AH: An everlasting supply of, er, English sausages, I love English sausages, and cheese.
I: You have had your luxury.
AH: I've had my luxury.

I: You'd have to make your own cheese from turtle milk or something. How long do you think you could endure it?

AH: How long could I survive on a desert island? Well, knowing my fortitude and my resilience, I'll probably give myself about two weeks.

I: If you could take only one disc of the eight you have chosen which would it be?

AH: I think I would take 'Myfanwy', Triorchy Male Voice Choir.

I: And you've told us your luxury - that's going to be a piano.

AH: Yes

I: One book. You have The Bible and the complete works of Shakespeare already for you on the island.

AH: I'd take *The Great Gatsby*.

I: *The Great Gatsby?*

AH: Yes, I've read it a few times and I find it a haunting book.

I: Who's it by?

AH: F Scott Fitzgerald.

I: Right. *The Great Gatsby* by F Scott Fitzgerald. And thank you, Anthony Hopkins, for letting us hear your desert island discs.

AH: Thank you.

English in action: 3
See the Teacher's Book, Unit 18

UNIT 19
Exercise 6 Listening: 2

C: Hi, Rick from Hackney in London. Are you on the line?

R: Yes. Hi.

C: How can I help you?

R: Well, I'm in a bit of a mess.

C: That's what I'm here for. Do you want to tell me about it? Take your time.

R: Well, you see I met this girl on holiday in Tenerife and I really like her.

C: Well that sounds OK. What's the problem?

R: Well. It's stupid really. But I thought she wouldn't be interested in me so I said I was French.

C: To make yourself more interesting?

R: Yes, and you know I did a bit of French at school and I can't say much but I can do 'a good French accent.'

C: Yeah. Not bad at all.

R: Well, she believed me and it just sort of went on like that and I didn't think much about it. I told her my name was Pierre and I lived in Marseilles in the south of France. It was a bit of a laugh really.

C: Yeah.

R: Well, we got on really well, had a great holiday and then we went back to England. Except I said I was going back to France.

C: Uh huh.

R: She lives up north near Manchester and I live in . . .

C: In Hackney, London.

R: Yeah right. Well, we wanted to keep in contact, so I said I'd phone her.

C: Right.

R: Anyway, I said she couldn't phone me. I told her I had a new flat and I didn't have a phone and. . .

C: Got it.

R: Well, I wanted to see her again so I phoned and said I was coming to England, for my job you know, and she invited me to meet her family.

C: In Manchester?

R: Yeah.

C: And they realised the truth?

R: No. No. They liked me.

C: Still with your French accent?

R: Yes.

C: Uh huh.

R: In fact, they took me really seriously. They asked my advice about the wine and everything.

C: I see. You are in a bit of a fix aren't you.

R: Yeah. Well that's just it. What do I do now? I really like her. I really like them. I think they like me. What should I do?

Exercise 6 Listening: 6

C: I see. You are in a bit of a fix aren't you.

R: Yeah. Well that's just it. What do I do now? I really like her. I really like them. I think they like me. What should I do?

C: Well Rick. I think you know what to do, don't you?

R: Run! Run as far away as possible!

C: I don't think you really want to, do you? Or you wouldn't have rung me.

R: I suppose not.

C: Well, if I were you, I'd buy a big bunch of flowers and tell her the truth. I certainly wouldn't tell any more lies. She can only tell . . .

UNIT 20
Thinking about learning: Radio Magazine
For the complete tapescript of *Radio Magazine*, see Additional Tapescripts at the end of the Teacher's Book.

The Thirty-Nine Steps

A man is walking down some steps. Ten, eleven, twelve. He walks down the steps, and he is counting. He is counting the steps. Thirty-six, thirty-seven, thirty-eight. The man stops. He has a small black notebook in his hand. He writes in the notebook: *39 steps.*

The next day, Scudder is talking to two men. They are Lord Harkness and Porton. 'Lord Harkness,' Scudder says. 'There are spies in London. The spies want a war – a war in Europe! We must stop them!'

'A war?' Lord Harkness says. 'Oh, no, Scudder.'

'Please listen to me,' Scudder says. 'You are Members of Parliament. You can help. These men have a plan. I know the plan – I have it in my notebook here. They want a war in Europe.'

'What is this plan?' Porton asks. 'And who are these men?'

'Well, I don't know their names – their English names. But they aren't English. They are spies.'

The three men are talking, and they can't see another man. But there is another man, too. He is watching them – watching and listening.

'You must believe me!' Scudder is saying now. 'We are in danger. Europe is in danger!' Scudder is shouting.

'And these spies – what are they going to do?' Lord Harkness asks. He looks at Porton and he smiles. 'You see spies everywhere Scudder.'

'Listen. On the fifteenth, Karolides is coming to London,' Scudder says. 'He's going to speak in Parliament.'

'The Greek Prime Minister?' Porton asks. He is listening now.

'Yes,' Scudder says. 'Karolides can stop the war. They know that. And they want the war. On the fifteenth, they are going to kill him!'

Lord Harkness gets up. 'I'm sorry, Scudder,' he says. 'But I don't believe you.'

The next day, Scudder is walking along the street. He sees a newspaper. LORD HARKNESS MURDERED the newpaper says.

'Murdered?' Scudder thinks. 'Dead? Oh, no! Where is Porton? I'm going to find Porton!'

Porton is coming out of his club. He is coming down the steps, and Appleton is beside him. Appleton is another Member of Parliament. Porton and Appleton stop in front of the club. They are talking. Scudder sees them, and he runs towards them. 'Porton!' he shouts. 'Porton, be careful! Lord Harkness is dead – murdered! Be careful!'

Then there is a noise from a high window above them. Porton looks up. Then another noise. A shot! It's the noise of a gun. And another shot. Porton falls to the ground – dead! Scudder runs to him. People are screaming, running. 'Stop! Stop!' a policeman shouts. 'Appleton!' Scudder shouts. He looks round. But – where is Appleton? He isn't there.

Mini-dictionary

This Mini-dictionary contains the most important words in *The Pre-Intermediate Choice*. For a more complete list of the groups of words below, please see the following pages.
- alphabet 6
- shops 75
- parts of the body 4, 15, 63
- food 96
- types of music 111
- rooms of the house 106–7
- means of transport 20
- work and leisure activities 8, 20, 27
- animals 94

The Mini-dictionary contains definitions from the *Longman New Junior English dictionary*.

Abbreviations: *n.* noun; *adj.* adjective; *v.* verb; *adv.* adverb; *pron.* pronoun; *prep.* preposition; *pl.* plural.
/ ' / shows main stress.
/ ' / or / ʷ/ at the end of a word means that this sound is usually pronounced when the next word begins with a vowel sound.

Phonemic chart

Consonants				Vowels		
/p/	pen	/s/	son	/iː/	eat	/eɪ/	say
/b/	bed	/z/	cheese	/ɪ/	sit	/əʊ/	no
/t/	tall	/ʃ/	shop	/e/	egg	/aɪ/	my
/d/	day	/ʒ/	television	/æ/	taxi	/aʊ/	how
/k/	car	/h/	hot	/ɑː/	far	/ɔɪ/	boy
/g/	go	/m/	man	/ɒ/	chocolate	/ɪə/	here
		/n/	finish	/ɔː/	door	/eə/	where
/tʃ/	chair	/ŋ/	sing	/ʊ/	book	/ʊə/	tourist
/dʒ/	jam	/l/	look	/uː/	shoe		
		/r/	read	/ʌ/	bus		
/f/	four	/j/	young	/ɜː/	shirt		
/v/	very	/w/	walk	/ə/	butter		
/θ/	think						
/ð/	this						

Numbers are page numbers. LR means Language Review.

accountant /əˈkaʊntənt/ *n.* a person whose job it is to keep lists of money spent and money earned for people or companies. p25

advertisement /ədˈvɜːtɪsmənt/ *n.* a notice in a newspaper, on a wall or on TV to encourage people to buy goods. p19

advice /ədˈvaɪs/ *n.* (no *pl.*) suggestion to someone about what they should do. *He never takes my* **advice** (= He never does what I tell him.). **advise** *v.* p27

affectionate /əˈfekʃnət/ *adj.* feeling or showing love. p94

agree /əˈgriː/ *v.* to think the same as someone else: *I* **agree** *with you.* p110

airport /ˈeəpɔːt/ *n.* a place where aeroplanes land and take off. p20

alarm clock /əˈlɑːm klɒk/ *n.* a clock that rings a bell at the time you want to wake up. p18

ambition /æmˈbɪʃn/ *n.* a strong wish to be successful. **ambitious/unambitious** *adj.* p13

amused/amusing /əˈmjuːzd, əˈmjuːzɪŋ/ *adj.* to feel/to make you feel like laughing. *I was* **amused** *by her story; it was* **amusing***.* p41/42

annoyed /əˈnɔɪd/ *adj.* feeling a little angry: *I was* **annoyed** *because I missed the bus.* p111

answer phone /ˈɑːnsə fəʊn/ *n.* a machine which records messages when no-one answers the phone: *If I'm not in when you ring, leave a message on my* **answer phone***.* p108

appearance /əˈpɪərəns/ *n.* what someone/something looks like: *You shouldn't judge people only by their* **appearance***.* p15

applaud /əˈplɔːd/ *v.* to strike the hands together to show pleasure at something: *Everyone* **applauded** *when the play ended.* p57

army /ˈɑːmɪ/ *n.* (*pl.* **armies**) a lot of soldiers fighting together. p87

article /ˈɑːtɪkl/ *n.* a piece of writing in a newspaper or magazine. *I read an interesting* **article** *about Germany today.* p7

artist /ˈɑːtɪst/ *n.* a person who paints, draws or produces pieces of art. p13

aspirin /ˈæsprɪn/ *n.* a medicine (a pill or tablet) that makes pain go away. p75

attractive /əˈtræktɪv/ *adj.* pleasing, especially to look at (applies to men and women). p15

audience /ˈɔːdɪəns/ *n.* all the people watching a play, listening to music at a concert, etc. p57

band /bænd/ *n.* a small group of people who play music together. p57

bar /bɑːʳ/ *n.*
1 a piece of material such as soap or chocolate. p96
2 a place where you can buy and consume alcoholic drink and sometimes food. p55

beautiful /ˈbjuːtɪfəl/ *adj.* very good-looking (usually of women), very pleasing: *What a* **beautiful** *day!* p15

behaviour /bɪˈheɪvjəʳ/ *n.* (no *pl.*) the way you act: *He got out of prison two years early for good* **behaviour***.* p34

belt /belt/ *n.* a piece of cloth or leather worn round the middle of the body: *I need a* **belt** *to keep up my trousers.* p91

bicycle /ˈbaɪsɪkl/ *n.* (or **cycle** or **bike**) a machine with two wheels for riding on. p69

bill /bɪl/ *n.* a piece of paper showing how much you must pay for something: *At the end of the meal I asked the waiter for the* **bill***.* p25

birth /bɜːθ/ *n.* being born; being brought into the world: *My sister* **gave birth** *to a girl yesterday.* p67

birthday /ˈbɜːθdeɪ/ *n.* the day of the year on which a person was born. p74

blouse /blaʊz/ *n.* a loose piece of clothing for women, reaching from the neck to about the waist. p34

body /ˈbɒdɪ/ *n.* (*pl.* **bodies**) the whole of a person or animal, but not the mind. p4 (for different parts of the body see p15 + 63)

bored/boring /bɔːd, ˈbɔːrɪŋ/ *adj.* to feel/ to make you feel tired and uninterested. *I was* **bored** *because the job was so* **boring***.* p41/42

borrow /ˈbɒrəʊ/ *v.* to get the use of something which you are going to give back later: *I've left my pen at home; can I* **borrow** *yours?* p60

bottle /ˈbɒtl/ *n.* a tall, round glass or plastic container, with a narrow neck: *a milk* **bottle***.* p96

box /bɒks/ *n.* (*pl.* **boxes**) a container with stiff straight sides, made from wood, cardboard, plastic or metal: *a box of matches.* p96

brave /breɪv/ *adj.* without fear, or not showing it: *It was very* **brave** *of you to save the child from the fire.* p94

briefcase /ˈbriːfkeɪs/ *n.* a thin flat bag for papers or books. See picture p18

bury /ˈberɪ/ *v.* to put or hide something in the ground. p94

bus stop /ˈbʌstɒp/ *n.* a place where buses stop for people to get on and off. p20

buy /baɪ/ *v.* to get something by giving money for it: *I* **bought** *a new radio yesterday.* p62

call /kɔːl/ *v.* to name: *They decided to* **call** *their new baby John.* p31

can /kæn/
1 *v.* to know how to; be able to: **Can** *she swim? No, she can't.* p4
2 *n.* (or **tin**) a container made of metal: *Please buy some* **cans** *of tomato soup from the shop.* p96

camera /ˈkæmrə/ *n.* an instrument for taking photographs. p18

cane /keɪn/ *n.* a long thin stick used to hit children at some schools. p91

careful /ˈkeəfəl/ *adj.* thinking about something, paying attention: *Be* **careful** *when you cross the road.* p94

cartoon /kɑːˈtuːn/ *n.* a film made by photographing drawings. *I like the Mickey Mouse* **cartoons** *best.* p44

cash /kæʃ/
1 *v.* to get coins or paper money in exchange for a cheque: *Can I* **cash** *this cheque please?* p98
2 *n.* (no *pl.*) coins and paper money.

catch /kætʃ/ v. to get transport: *I caught the train to Dover.* p20

certificate /sə'tɪfɪkət/ n. a written paper saying something important: *Your birth certificate tells people when you were born.* p51

change /tʃeɪndʒ/ v. to become or make different: *This town has changed since I was a child.* **change** n.: *to make a change (in lifestyle)* p86

character /'kærəktə'/ n. what a person or thing is like: *He has a strong but gentle character.* p15

cheap /tʃiːp/ adj. costing only a little money: *A bicycle is much cheaper than a car.* p61

cheer /tʃɪə'/ v. to shout because you are pleased. p37

cheese /tʃiːz/ n. a food made from thickened milk. p96

cheque /tʃɔk/ n. a printed piece of paper from a cheque book which you write on, and which can be exchanged for money at a bank. p98

choose /tʃuːz/ v. to decide which of a number of things you want: *She chose to study chemistry rather than biology.* p21

chop /tʃɒp/ n. a cut of meat, usually containing a bone: *A lamb chop comes from a young sheep.* p75

city /'sɪtɪ/ n. (pl. cities) a large town. p20

clever /'klevə'/ adj. quick at learning and understanding things: *He wasn't very clever at school but he is clever with his hands and makes beautiful furniture.* p25

cliff /klɪf/ n. an area of high, steep rock, often close to the sea. See picture p101

climate /'klaɪmɪt/ n. (no pl.) the weather that a place has. *The climate in Ecuador is tropical.* p30

clothes /kləʊðz/ pl. n. things we wear. See examples p13

coach /kəʊtʃ/ n. a type of bus that goes between towns: *She caught the coach from Manchester coach station and went to Glasgow.* p20

colleague /'kɒliːg/ n. a person who works with you especially in a profession. p9

comedy /'kɒmədɪ/ n. a funny play, film, etc. that makes us laugh. p44

compact disc or **CD** /kɒmpæk'dɪsk/ n. a type of record with very high quality sound played on a special machine. See picture p49

complain /kəm'pleɪn/ v. to say that something is not good, or that you are unhappy or angry with something: *We complained about the bad food.* **complaint** n. p117

computer /kəm'pjuːtə'/ n. a machine that can store information and work out answers quickly: *All our information is stored on a computer.* p108

concert /'kɒnsət/ n. pop or classical music played for a lot of people. p57

confident /'kɒnfɪdənt/ adj. feeling sure or safe: *I was confident that I had passed the examination.* p13

cook /kʊk/ v. to make food ready by heating it: *I haven't finished cooking the dinner yet.* p63

cooker /'kʊkə'/ n. a machine for cooking food. p108

cosmetic /kɒz'metɪk/ adj. intended to make your skin or body more beautiful: **cosmetic** surgery. p15

cost /kɒst/ v. to have as a price: *How much did that bag cost? It cost £50!* p10

country /'kʌntrɪ/ n.
1 (pl. countries) an area ruled by one government: *France and Germany are European countries.* p20
2 (no pl.) the land that is not a town: *He lives in the country.* p82

creative /krɪ'eɪtɪv/ adj. creating new and original ideas and things: *They are a creative couple; she paints and he writes novels.* p25

credit card /'kredɪt kɑːd/ n. a card which allows you to get goods and services without using coins or notes. p98

cricket /'krɪkɪt/ n. a team game played with ball, bat and wickets (popular in Britain). p37

criminal /'krɪmɪnl/ n. a person who does something wrong and punishable by law. p54

crisps /krɪsps/ n. thin pieces of potato cooked in very hot oil and often eaten as a snack with drinks. p75

cruel /'kruːəl/ adj. liking to hurt other people or animals. p94

curly /'kɜːlɪ/ adj. to roll or bend in a round shape, not straight: *She has very curly hair.* p15

current account /kʌrənt ə'kaʊnt/ n. a bank account from which money can be taken out immediately by cheque or using a card. p98

dark /dɑːk/ adj. of a deep colour, nearer black than white; not fair or light: *He had dark hair.* p15

dead /ded/ adj. not living: *My grand-mother has been dead for ten years.* p67

death /deθ/ n. being dead or dying, the opposite of birth: *Her father's death was very sudden.* **die** v. p67

decide /dɪ'saɪd/ v. to choose what to do: *I decided to go home and not to the cinema.* **decision** n. p19

definitely /'defɪnɪtlɪ/ adv. with no doubt: *He'll definitely be home by six o'clock.* p50

dentist /'dentɪst/ n. a doctor who looks after your teeth. p4

depressed/depressing /dɪ'prest, dɪ'presɪŋ/ adj. to feel/make you feel very sad or miserable. *She felt depressed after watching the film; it was depressing.* p41/42

desert island /dezət 'aɪlənd/ n. a small area of uninhabited land surrounded by water: *Robinson Crusoe lived on a desert island for many years.* p111

diary /'daɪərɪ/ n. (pl. diaries) a book in which you write things that have happened or things to remember each day. p27

die /daɪ/ v. to stop living: *She died of her illness.* **dead** adj. **death** n. p67

different /'dɪfrənt/ adj. not the same: *Her character is quite different from her brother's – she's kind and he's nasty.* p13

dirty /'dɜːtɪ/ adj. not clean: *My shoes were very dirty after working in the garden.* p94

disagree /dɪsə'griː/ v. to think differently from someone else: *I disagree with you.* p110

disappointed/disappointing /dɪsə'pɔɪntɪd, dɪsə'pɔɪntɪŋ/ adj. to feel/to make you feel unhappy because something is not as good as you hoped. *She was disappointed because her exam results were poor and disappointing.* p41/42

disgusted/disgusting /dɪs'gʌstɪd, dɪs'gʌstɪŋ/ adj. to feel/to make you feel strong dislike and sometimes physically ill. *We were disgusted by the bad service and disgusting food.* p41/42

dishwasher /'dɪʃwɒʃə'/ n. a machine for doing the washing up: *After the meal, they put the dirty plates in the dishwasher.* p108

divorce /dɪ'vɔːs/ v. to arrange by law for a husband and wife to separate. *I divorced my wife last year.* **divorced** adj. p67

draw /drɔː/ v. to make a picture, especially with a pencil or pen: *She drew (a picture of) the flowers in that vase.* p76

dress up /dres'ʌp/ v. to put on nice, special clothes: *She dressed up to go for her interview.* p24

drive /draɪv/ v. to make a vehicle move in the direction you want: *Can you drive (a car)?* p63

drop /drɒp/ v. to fall or let fall: *She dropped her keys on the floor.* p94

each other /iːtʃ'ʌðə'/ pron. each person does the same thing to the other: *Susan and Robert kissed each other.* p15

earn /ɜːn/ v. to get money in return for work: *He has earned a lot of money by working in the evenings.* p10

earthquake /'ɜːθkweɪk/ n. a strong and sudden shaking of the ground. p73

easy /'iːzɪ/
1 adj. not difficult: *The exam was easy; she passed easily.*
2 adv. without much effort: *Take it easy, relax!* p86

elect /ɪ'lekt/ v. to choose, usually by vote: *The government is made up of men and women elected by the people of the country.* **elected** adj. **election** n. p79

embarrassed/embarrassing /ɪm'bærəst, ɪm'bærəsɪŋ/ adj. to feel/to make you feel stupid in front of other people. *I was embarrassed by her embarrassing behaviour in front of my family.* p72

emigrate /'emɪgreɪt/ v. to leave your country in order to go and live in another country. p70

emperor /'emprə'/ n. (fem. empress) a ruler of a country/countries. p78

employ /ɪm'plɔɪ/ v. to give work to: *The National Bank employs a great many people.* **employed** adj. **employment** n. p67

enjoy /ɪn'dʒɔɪ/ v. to get pleasure from: *I enjoy playing tennis.* p8

examination /ɪgzæmɪ'neɪʃn/ n. (abbrev. exam) a test of knowledge: *Did you pass the exam you took last month?* p51

excited/exciting /ɪk'saɪtɪd, ɪk'saɪtɪŋ/ adj. to have/to cause strong feelings of expectation or happiness. *The children were excited and couldn't sleep. The idea of seeing Santa Claus was so exciting.* p41/42

expensive /ɪk'spensɪv/ adj. costing a lot of money: *It is expensive to travel by plane.* p61

extravagant /ɪk'strævəgənt/ adj. spending too much money: *He's very extravagant, he spends all his money on clothes.* p62

fail /feɪl/ v. not to do well, or not to do what you intend: *He failed his English* exam so he retook it the next year. p51

fair /feə'/ *adj.*
1 equally good to everyone; just: *It is not* **fair** *that my brother got a bicycle and I didn't.* p25
2 light in colour, not dark: *She has very* **fair** *hair.* p15

faithful /'feɪθfəl/ *adj.* able to be trusted: *He's a very* **faithful** *friend.* p94

false /fɔːls/ *adj.* not true or real: *My grandfather has to wear* **false** *teeth.* p49

feel /fiːl/ *v.*
1 to experience a sensation: *I* **feel** *ill.* p9
2 to recognise something by touch: *I can't see in the dark but it* **feels** *like a key.* p63

fight /faɪt/ *v.* an attempt by two or more people to hurt or kill each other: *The police were called to stop a group of men* **fighting** *outside a pub.* p91

figure /'fɪgə'/ *n.* the shape of the body. p15

find /faɪnd/ *v.* to see or get something after looking for it: *After looking in every room for my glasses, I* **found** *them in the kitchen.* p60

fish /fɪʃ/ *n.* (*pl.* **fish** or **fishes**) a cold-blooded animal that lives in water. p64

fit /fɪt/ *adj.* in good physical condition: *I'm not very* **fit**. *I must do more exercise.* p25

flatter /'flætə'/ *v.* to say that someone is better, nicer, etc. than they really are: *She never stops* **flattering** *me, she says I'm wonderful!* p94

flower /'flaʊə'/ *n.* the part of a plant which holds the seeds and which is usually brightly-coloured: *We have lots of beautiful* **flowers** *in the garden.* p15

food /fuːd/ *n.* (no *pl.*) what you eat: *Is there enough* **food** *in the fridge?* See examples. p96

football /'fʊtbɔːl/ *n.* a game, sometimes called soccer, in which two teams try to kick the ball into each other's goal. p37

foreign currency /fɒrən'kʌrənsɪ/ *n.* money used in another country: *We must get some* **foreign currency** *from the bank before we go on holiday.* p18

forget /fə'get/ *v.* not to remember: *Don't* **forget** *to post the letters!* p72

freezer /'friːzə'/ *n.* a machine that keeps food very cold, below 0°C, so that it keeps fresh for a long time. p108

fridge /frɪdʒ/ *n.* a machine for keeping food cold and fresh: *Put the milk in the* **fridge** *when you have finished breakfast.* p108

friend /frend/ *n.* a person you like and feel you can trust. **friendly/unfriendly** *adj.*

frightened/frightening /'fraɪtnd, 'fraɪtnɪŋ/ *adj.* the state of being afraid. *I was* **frightened** *of being alone in the house at night after watching the* **frightening** *horror film.* p41/42

garden /'gɑːdn/ *n.* a place where trees, flowers or vegetables are grown, round a house or in a public place: *She moved to a house with a* **garden**. p64

generous /'dʒenrəs/ *adj.* giving what you can, opposite of *mean*: *It was very* **generous** *of you to lend them your new car to go on holiday.* p55

get /get/ *v.*
1 to receive: *I* **got** *a book for my*

---

birthday. p69
2 to buy: *Go to the supermarket and* **get** *some food.* p75
3 to become: *He* **got** *married in June.* p48
4 to arrive: *He* **got** *home late from work.* p50
5 to enter/leave transport: *She* **got** *on/off the bus. He* **got** *into/out of the car.* p20

glass /glɑːs/ *n.* (*pl.* **glasses**) a cup made of glass without a handle. p55

glasses /'glɑːsɪz/ (no *sing.*) glass or plastic worn in front of the eyes to help people see better. See picture p18

give up /gɪv'ʌp/ *v.* to stop: *I* **gave up** *smoking last week.* p108

go away /gəʊ'ə'weɪ/ *v.* to leave: *Please* **go away** *and leave me alone.* p86

government /'gʌvəmənt/ *n.* the people who control what happens in a country. **govern** *v.* p79

grade /greɪd/ *n.* a certain level, size or quality: *I need good* **grades** *in my exams to get to university.* p51

graveyard /'greɪvjɑːd/ *n.* a place where dead people are buried. See picture p67

hairdresser /'heədresə'/ *n.* the person who cuts and shapes hair. p25

happen /'hæpən/ *v.* to take place, to be: *The accident* **happened** *outside my house.* p54

hardworking /hɑːd'wɜːkɪŋ/ *adj.* not *lazy*: *They are a very* **hardworking** *family, they never take a holiday.* p14

hat /hæt/ *n.* something you wear on your head. p13

hate /heɪt/ *v.* to not like strongly. *I* **hate** *living in the city.* p37

headache /'hedeɪk/ *n.* pain in your head: *Can I have an aspirin. I have a very bad* **headache**. p117

health /helθ/ *n.* (no *pl.*) the state of your body; how you are: *His general* **health** *is not very good, he is often ill.* **healthy** *adj.* p67

hear /hɪə'/ *v.* to get sounds through the ears: *I* **heard** *the rain on the roof.* p40

heavy /'hevɪ/ *adj.* weighing a lot, not light: *Can you help me? This bag is very* **heavy**. p13

help /help/ *v.* to do something or part of something for someone: *I can't lift this box – will you* **help** *me?* p24

high /haɪ/ *adj.* tall or far from the ground: *The* **highest** *mountain in Africa is Mount Kilimanjaro. It is nearly 9000m* **high**. p20

history /'hɪstrɪ/ *n.* (no *pl.*) the study of the past: *I always enjoyed my* **history** *lessons at school.* p51

hobby /'hɒbɪ/ *n.* something you do to amuse yourself in your free time: *My favourite* **hobby** *is collecting stamps.* p38

holiday /'hɒlɪdeɪ/ *n.* a time when you do not work or go to school: *We went to Spain for our summer* **holidays**. p9

homework /'həʊmwɜːk/ *n.* work given to you at school to be done at home. p27

honeymoon /'hʌnɪmuːn/ *n.* a holiday taken by people who have just got married: *They went to Brazil for their* **honeymoon**. p48

horror film /'hɒrə fɪlm/ *n.* a frightening film, often violent: *The best* **horror film** *I have ever seen is Dracula!* p44

housework /'haʊswɜːk/ *n.* work done to keep your home clean and tidy

---

including washing floors, cleaning windows, ironing, etc. p5

hungry /'hʌŋgrɪ/ *adj.* the feeling of wanting to eat: *I'm really* **hungry**, *I haven't eaten anything all day!* p29

identical /aɪ'dentɪkl/ *adj.* exactly the same: *The two cups are* **identical**, *they are the same size, shape and colour.* p13

ill /ɪl/ *adj.* not feeling healthy; unwell: *She can't go to school because she is* **ill**. **illness** *n.* p67

immigration /ɪmɪ'greɪʃn/ *n.* the process of entering another country to make your life and home there. **immigrant** *n.* the person who immigrates. p70

independent /ɪndɪ'pendənt/ *adj.* able to look after yourself: *She's a very* **independent** *person, she rarely needs anybody else.* p13

inherit /ɪn'herɪt/ *v.* to get something from somebody else when they die: *He* **inherited** *the house when his grandmother died.* p67

intelligent /ɪn'telɪdʒənt/ *adj.* having powers of reasoning and understanding: *Mike is a very* **intelligent** *young man. He passed all his exams.* p45

interested/interesting /'ɪntrəstɪd, 'ɪntrəstɪŋ/ *adj.* to want/to make you want to find out more about something. *He was* **interested** *in maths because the lessons were so* **interesting**. p42

interview /'ɪntəvjuː/ *n.* a meeting to decide if a person is suitable for a job, or to ask her/his opinions: *I'm going for an* **interview** *for the job of Financial Controller today.* p27

jacket /'dʒækɪt/ *n.* a short coat with sleeves. p35

jar /dʒɑː'/ *n.* a container like a bottle with a short neck and a wide opening: *Could you pass me that* **jar** *of jam?* p96

joke /dʒəʊk/ *n.* something you say or do to make people laugh: *She told us a* **joke** *but it wasn't funny.* p60

just /dʒʌst/ *adv.* a very short time: *I arrived* **just** *after the bus left, it was very annoying!* p41

kettle /'ketl/ *n.* a metal pot specially for boiling water. p108

king /kɪŋ/ *n.* a male ruler of a country, a monarch. p78

kiss /kɪs/ *v.* to touch someone with the lips, as a sign of love or liking: *He always* **kissed** *his wife when he said goodbye.* p36

lady /'leɪdɪ/ *n.* (*pl.* **ladies**) a polite word for a woman. p95

large /lɑːdʒ/ *adj.* big; able to hold a lot: *They need a* **large** *house because they have nine children.* p15

late /leɪt/ *adj./adv.* after the usual or agreed time: *I was* **late** *getting up and arrived* **late**. p27

laugh /lɑːf/ *v.* to make a sound that shows you are pleased, happy or think something is funny: *We all* **laughed** *a lot when she told us the joke.* p60

law /lɔː/ *n.* a rule made by the government which all people must obey: *It is against the* **law** *to drive over 70 mph on the motorway in Britain.* p79

lawyer /'lɔːjə'/ *n.* a person who advises people about laws and represents them in court. p79

lazy /'leɪzɪ/ *adj.* not wanting to work; not hardworking: *She is very* **lazy**. *She never works.* p13

lead /liːd/ *v.* to show the way. p79

leader /'liːdə'/ *n.* the person who gives direction to others: *He is the greatest* **leader** *this country has ever had.*   p79

leave /liːv/ *v.* to go away from: *This train will* **leave** *for Manchester in 15 minutes.*   p51

lie /laɪ/ *n.* something which is not true: *He told a* **lie** *when he said he didn't know her name.*   p91

like /laɪk/
1 *v.* to find pleasant; enjoy: *I* **like** *all sports and particularly going to football matches.*   p8
2 *prep.* similar to something or someone in some way: *She looks* **like** *her mother but she is more* **like** *her father in character.*   p15

look /lʊk/ *v.*
1 to point the eyes towards something: **Look** *at the blackboard.* p6
2 to seem to be: *That dog* **looks** *dangerous.*
3 to care for: *She* **looks** *after her sister after school.*   p27

look like /'lʊk laɪk/ *v.* to have a similar appearance: *I* **look like** *my brother.*   p15

long /lɒŋ/ *adj.* not short; *She's got* **long** *black hair.*   p20

love /lʌv/ *v.* to like something or someone very much: *I* **love** *this book, it's fantastic!* p8

love story /'lʌv stɔːrɪ/ *n.* a book or film about love: *Gone With The Wind is a* **love story**.   p44

lunch /lʌntʃ/ *n.* the meal you eat in the middle of the day.   p72

luxury /'lʌkʃərɪ/ *n.* (*pl.* **luxuries**) something that you do not really need, but that is very nice: *Going to school by car is a* **luxury**.   p111

magazine /mægə'ziːn/ *n.* a large, thin paper-covered publication containing stories, articles and pictures.   p10

make a change /meɪk ə'tʃeɪndʒ/ *v.* to change things, particularly your lifestyle.   p86

manage /'mænɪdʒ/ *v.* to have power and control over someone or something: *I* **manage** *the Sales Department.* **manager** *n.* the person.   p25

management /'mænɪdʒmənt/ *n.* the group of people who control a business.   p26

map /mæp/ *n.* a flat drawing of a large area: *In the library there are* **maps** *of towns, countries and the world.*   p18

marry /'mærɪ/ *v.* to take someone as a husband or wife: *She* **married** *him in church.* **married** *adj.*   p48

marriage /'mærɪdʒ/ *n.* the occasion when people are married: *My sister's* **marriage** *took place in church.*   p120

match /mætʃ/
1 *v.* to be like something else in size, shape, etc.: *These shoes do not* **match** *this jacket, they are the wrong colour.* p13
2 *n.* a game between two people or two teams. *We saw a good football* **match** *on TV this afternoon.* p37
3 *n.* a small stick you can use to light other things: *I need some* **matches** *to light this fire with.* p96

meal /miːl/ *n.* the food we eat at regular times: *She cooked a delicious* **meal** *last night.* p32

meat /miːt/ *n.* (*no pl.*) the parts of an animal's body used as food: *I don't eat*

meat, *I'm a vegetarian.* p75

medium /'miːdjəm/ *adj.* not big or small!; of middle size or amount: *She is* **medium** *height.*   p15

meet /miːt/ *v.* to come together: *Let's* **meet** *at your house tonight.*   p40

Member of Parliament /membərəv'pɑːləmənt/ *n.* (or M.P.) elected member of the British Government.   p79

memory /'memrɪ/ *n.* the ability to remember things: *I've got a very good* **memory** *for names.*   p72

microwave (oven) /'maɪkrəweɪv/ *n.* a machine which cooks food very quickly by radiation.   p108

middle-aged /mɪdl'eɪdʒd/ *adj.* someone between about 40 and 60 years old.   p85

military service /mɪlɪtrɪ'sɜːvɪs/ *n.* the time when people have to be part of the army of their country, often one year after leaving school.   p87

Mormon /'mɔːmən/ *n.* member of a particular religious group originally formed in the USA.   p87

mountain /'maʊntɪn/ *n.* A very high hill: *Mount Everest is the highest* **mountain** *in the world.*   p20

move /muːv/ *v.* to go from one place to another; to change where you live: *They* **moved** *from New York to Paris last year.* p66

murder /'mɜːdə'/ *v.* to kill a person unlawfully. **murderer** *n.* the person who kills.   p102

need /niːd/ *v.* to not have something that is necessary: *I* **need** *some money to go to the shops.* p96

novel /'nɒvəl/ *n.* a long written story usually printed as a book.   p74

nurse /nɜːs/ *n.* a person who is trained to help a doctor and look after people who are ill.   p25

obsession /əb'seʃn/ *n.* something you cannot stop thinking about: *Cleaning has become an* **obsession** *of mine: I wash the floor twice a day.* **obsessive** *adj.* p34

opposition /ɒpə'zɪʃn/ *n.* the political party who are not in power: *As expected, the* **opposition** *disagreed with the government's decision.* **oppose** *v.*   p79

order (a meal) /'ɔːdə'/ *v.* to say what you want: *We* **ordered** *a bottle of red wine to drink with the meal.* p32

organise /'ɔːgənaɪz/ *v.* to arrange in a careful way, put in order, plan: *Jane* **organised** *the party: she bought all the food, chose the music and sent out invitations.* **organised** *adj.* p25

owner /'əʊnə'/ *n.* the person which something belongs to: *Who is the* **owner** *of that red car?* **own** *v.* p40

packet /'pækɪt/ *n.* a small container or parcel: *Have you got another* **packet** *of cigarettes?* p96

pair /peə'/ *n.* two things/people which are alike or joined together: *a* **pair** *of shoes.* p13

parliament /'pɑːləmənt/ *n.* a large group of people elected by the people of the country to make laws.   p79

party /'pɑːtɪ/ *n.*
1 a meeting of friends to enjoy themselves, eat, drink, listen to music etc.: *We are going to Jessie's birthday* **party** *tonight.* p27
2 a group of people with the same

political views: *Are you a member of the* **Labour** *Party?* p80

pass /pɑːs/ *v.* to succeed in a test or examination: *It's fantastic. I've* **passed** *my driving test!* p51

passport /'pɑːspɔːt/ *n.* a little book with your photograph and facts about you in it, which you must have if you go to other countries.   p18

patient /'peɪʃnt/ *adj.* the ability to wait for something calmly without getting annoyed; not impatient: *Please be* **patient**, *I won't be long.*   p55

personality /pɜːsə'nælɪtɪ/ *n.* the nature and character of a particular person: *Judith is very nice, she has a lovely* **personality**.   p15

pet /pet/ *n.* an animal you look after and keep in the house: *We have lots of* **pets**: *cats, dogs and fish.*   p30

petrol /'petrəl/ *n.* (*no pl.*) a liquid used in cars to make the engine work.   p64

piece /piːs/ *n.* a part of something or a single thing: *He took a small* **piece** *of cake.*   p96

platform /'plætfɔːm/ *n.* a part of a station where you get on and off trains: *The next train to Cardiff leaves from* **Platform** *11.*   p14

play /pleɪ/ *v.*
1 to take part in a game: *The children* **played** *football in the garden.*   p35
2 to make sounds on a musical instrument: *She enjoys* **playing** *the guitar in her free time.*   p57

poem /'pəʊɪm/ *n.* writing with regular lines and sounds that expresses something in powerful or beautiful language: *This is a very sad* **poem** *about war.*   p88

point /pɔɪnt/ *v.* to show, especially with a finger: *He* **pointed** *to the picture on the wall.*   p55

poison /'pɔɪzən/ *v.* to kill with poison, a dangerous substance if it gets into your body. **poison** *n.*   p102

polite /pə'laɪt/ *adj.* having a kind and respectful way of behaving; not rude: *It's not* **polite** *to point at people!*   p57

politics /'pɒlɪtɪks/ *pl. n.* the study of government; how countries should be governed. **political** *adj.*, **politician** *n.* the person.   p78

pop /pɒp/ *n.* (*no pl.*) music or songs that younger people often like to listen or dance to.   p13

porter /'pɔːtə'/ *n.* a person who carries bags or other things for people particularly at a railway station.   p25

possession /pə'zeʃn/ *n.* something that belongs to you: *He lives in a small flat and doesn't have many* **possessions**.   p69

poverty /'pɒvətɪ/ *n.* (*no pl.*) the state of being poor: *She lived in* **poverty** *all her life.*   p66

prefer /prɪ'fɜː'/ *v.* to like better: *Which of these two dresses do you* **prefer**? p8

present /'prezənt/ *n.* something you give to someone: *I'm going to give her a new watch as her birthday* **present**.   p61

president /'prezɪdənt/ *n.* the head of government in a country that does not have a king or queen.   p78

prime minister /praɪ 'mɪnɪstə'/ *n.* the head of government in certain countries.   p78

prince /prɪns/ *n.* (*fem.* **princess**) the son of a king or queen.   p78

probably /'prɒbəblɪ/ *adv.* a good chance of something happening; likely: *It will* **probably** *rain tomorrow.* p50

product /'prɒdʌkt/ *n.* things that are made: *Our company has brought out a new range of kitchen* **products**. p28

promise /'prɒmɪs/ *v.* to say you will do something: *She* **promised** *she would write to her parents.* p80

punctual /'pʌŋktʃʊəl/ *adj.* coming at the right time, not late: *It's very important to be* **punctual** *for work.* p25

punish /'pʌnɪʃ/ *v.* to make someone suffer for something they have done wrong: *The teacher* **punished** *the children by making them stay behind after school.* **punishment** *n.* p91

qualification /kwɒlɪfɪ'keɪʃn/ *n.* special skills or knowledge: *What* **qualifications** *do you need for this job?* p51

quality /'kwɒlətɪ/ *n.* (*pl.* **qualities**) a good part of someone's character. p25

queen /kwiːn/ *n.* the female ruler of a country: *The* **Queen** *of England lives in Buckingham Palace.* p79

receptionist /rɪ'sepʃnɪst/ *n.* a person who works in the reception of a business, hotel, etc. p25

redundancy /rɪ'dʌndənsɪ/ *n.* when you lose your job because there is not enough work: *There have been 200* **redundancies** *at that factory because of the economic recession.* **redundant** *adj.* p67

reference /'refrəns/ *n.* a letter written about your character and/or abilities to use to support applications for a new job: *She had excellent* **references**, *so we gave her the job.* p70

relationship /rɪ'leɪʃnʃɪp/ *n.* connection between two people or things: *My brother and I have a very good* **relationship**. p15

relax /rɪ'læks/ *v.* to not worry, become calm, rest: *I'm going to sit in this chair and* **relax** *for half an hour.* **relaxed** *adj.* p64

religion /rɪ'lɪdʒən/ *n.* a special set of beliefs in one or more gods: *Hinduism and Buddhism are Eastern* **religions**. **religious** *adj.* p61

remember /rɪ'membə'/ *v.* to keep in mind, not to forget: *Did you* **remember** *to feed the cats?* p72

remind /rɪ'maɪnd/ *v.* to make someone remember: **Remind** *me to write and thank my uncle for the present.* p74

ring /rɪŋ/ *v.*
1 to operate a bell: *He* **rang** *the front door bell several times but no one answered.* p42
2 to telephone: *I* **rang** *Paul last night and asked him to come over for dinner.* p42

river /'rɪvə'/ *n.* a continuous flow of water along a course to the sea: *The longest* **river** *in Africa is the Nile.* See picture p64

salt /sɔːlt/ *n.* (no *pl.*) a white chemical found in sea water, rocks, etc. which we add to our food to make it taste better: *I use a lot of* **salt** *and pepper in my cooking.* p64

same /seɪm/ *adj.* not different; alike in one or more ways: *Your pen is the* **same** *as mine.* p13

say /seɪ/ *v.* to speak something: *He* **said** *he wanted to go home.* p114

scandal /'skændl/ *n.* something which causes a lot of people to talk and show they do not approve: *There was a great* **scandal** *when we found out that the doctor had been sent to prison for stealing.* p43

school /skuːl/ *n.* a place of education for children. (**Primary school** = 5–10 years old; **secondary school** = 11–16 or 18 years old): *My children go to a* **state school** *because* **private schools** *are so expensive.* p51

science fiction /saɪəns'fɪkʃn/ *n.* stories or films about imaginary future worlds or imaginary scientific developments. p44

settle down /setl'daʊn/ *v.* to begin to lead a quieter, more regular life: *At the age of 30, he decided it was time to get married and* **settle down**. p86

shake /ʃeɪk/ *v.* to move quickly from side to side, up and down, etc.: *We* **shook** *the tree and some apples fell down.* p36

shave /ʃeɪv/ *v.* to take hair from the face or body by cutting it very close: *My father* **shaves** *with an electric shaver every day.* p73

shocked/shocking /ʃɒkt, 'ʃɒkɪŋ/ *adj.* to be unpleasantly surprised/to cause unpleasant surprise: *I was* **shocked** *by her death; the news of her death was* **shocking**. p42

shirt /ʃɜːt/ *n.* a piece of clothing that covers the upper part of the body and arms: *He wore a T-shirt under his* **shirt**. p13

shoot /ʃuːt/ *v.* to fire at and hit: *He* **shot** *the bird with his gun.* p102

short /ʃɔːt/ *adj.* not very tall; not long; *She was a* **short** *girl with* **short**, *brown hair.* p13

shy /ʃaɪ/ *adj.* rather afraid to be with other people, not confident: *When the children met the Queen they were too* **shy** *to speak.* p13

sing /sɪŋ/ *v.* to make music with the voice: *She likes* **singing** *songs in the bath.* **singer** *n.* the person. p36

slate /sleɪt/ *n.* a cleanable surface for writing on. p74

slim /slɪm/ *adj.* thin, not fat: *I'm not* **slim** *enough to wear these trousers, they're too tight!* p15

sly /slaɪ/ *adj.* clever in deceiving: *The fruit seller was* **sly** *– he put his best fruit in front but gave people bad fruit from behind.* p94

smack /smæk/ *v.* to hit (children) with the open hand: *He* **smacked** *the naughty child.* p90

smell /smel/ *v.* to give off a good or bad perfume: *This perfume* **smells** *like roses.* p63

smoke /sməʊk/ *v.* to use cigarettes, a pipe etc.: *You must stop* **smoking**, *it's not good for you.* p35

soap /səʊp/ *n.* an oily substance that cleans things when it is put with water: *She washed her hands with* **soap**. p96

sociable /'səʊʃəbl/ *adj.* enjoying being with other people; not unsociable: *He's very* **sociable**, *he loves going to parties.* p55

social worker /'səʊʃl wɜːkə'/ *n.* someone who works to improve bad social conditions and helps people in need. p25

soldier /'səʊldʒə'/ *n.* a member of an army. See picture p66

song /sɒŋ/ *n.* a piece of music with words for singing. p36

sophisticated /sə'fɪstɪkeɪtɪd/ *adj.* experienced in social life and behaviour: *She's a very* **sophisticated** *young woman.* p15

sound /saʊnd/ *v.* to make a noise: *That* **sounds** *like Mike's car.* p63

souvenir /suːvə'nɪə'/ *n.* a thing that is kept to remember a place or event. p40

space capsule /'speɪs kæpsjuːl/ *n.* a vehicle for people or things to travel in into space. p49

spend /spend/ *v.* to give money or time: *How much money did you* **spend** *at the shops today?* p96

sport /spɔːt/ *n.* games and exercises done for pleasure: *Football and basketball are team* **sports**. p37

stab /stæb/ *v.* to wound with a pointed weapon: *He* **stabbed** *the man with a knife and he had to go to hospital.* p102

stage /steɪdʒ/ *n.* a raised floor, usually in a theatre: *The play was acted on a* **stage**. p57

station /'steɪʃn/ *n.*
1 a place where buses or trains stop: *a railway* **station**/*a bus* **station**. p20
2 a building for some special work: *a police* **station**. p60

stay /steɪ/ *v.* to continue to be: *He* **stayed** *with his father when he was ill.* p85

steal /stiːl/ *v.* to take something that does not belong to you without asking for it: *He* **stole** *a shirt when the shop assistant wasn't looking.* p111

straight /streɪt/ *adj.* not bending or curly: *The Romans built very* **straight** *roads.* p15

stranger /'streɪndʒə'/ *n.* a person you do not know. p14

strict /strɪkt/ *adj.* severe, especially about behaviour: *Our teacher is very* **strict**, *we have to do exactly what she says.* p90

stupid /'stjuːpɪd/ *adj.* not clever, not intelligent: *That was a very* **stupid** *question.* p94

subject /'sʌbdʒekt/ *n.* something you study: *Maths was my favourite* **subject** *at school.* p51

suicide /'suːsaɪd/ *n.* the act of killing yourself: *She was so depressed she tried to* **commit suicide**. p102

sunbathe /'sʌnbeɪð/ *v.* to lie in the sun. p20

sunglasses /'sʌnglɑːsɪz/ pl. *n.* dark glasses you wear to protect your eyes from the sun. p18

suntan lotion /'sʌntæn ləʊʃn/ *n.* cream you put on your body to protect it from the sun. p18

supporter /sə'pɔːtə'/ *n.* a person who gives encouragement to another person or group: *He is a* **supporter** *of Manchester United football team.*

surprise /sə'praɪz/ *n.* something unexpected which happens or is arranged by other people: *It was a* **surprise** *to see Steve – I thought he was on holiday.* p14

swallow /'swɒləʊ/ *v.* to take food or drink down the throat and into the stomach: *She* **swallowed** *the medicine quickly.* p94

swear /sweə'/ *v.* to use bad language: *He was so angry that he* **swore** *at his brother.* p91

swim /swɪm/ *v.* to move through water by

using your arms and legs. *She* **swam** *across the river.* p63

take /teɪk/ *v.*
1 to move something to another place: *She* **took** *her walkman to France.* p18
2 to drive someone: *I'll* **take** *you to the station.* p19
3 to photograph: **Take** *a photo of that building.* p20
4 to sit (an exam): *He* **took** *his final exams last week. If he doesn't pass, he can* **retake** *them.* p51

take it easy /teɪkɪ'tiːzɪ/ *v.* to relax: **Take it easy** *for a few days, have a rest!* p86

take your time /teɪkjə'taɪm/ *v.* to go slowly: *He* **took his time** *before he answered the telephone – it rang 20 times.* p86

tall /tɔːl/ *adj.* having a certain height; not short: *Sara is 1m 80* **tall.** p13

tape /teɪp/ *n.* (also **cassette**) a length of narrow tape on which sounds have been recorded: *I am going to buy the new Michael Jackson* **tape** *today.* p57

taste /teɪst/ *v.* the special sense by which we know one food from another. *This white wine* **tastes** *fantastic. It* **tastes** *like Champagne.* p63

taxation /tæk'seɪʃn/ *n.* (no *pl.*) the collection of money in tax by the government. p80

taxi rank /'tæksɪræŋk/ *n.* the official place to wait for taxis. p20

tell /tel/ *v.* to speak to or advise someone: *to* **tell the truth/lies.** p117

tennis player /'tenɪs pleɪə'/ *n.* a person who plays tennis: *John McEnroe is my favourite* **tennis player.** p25

terrible /'terəbl/ *adj.* very bad, awful: *I've got a* **terrible** *headache.* p9

thin /θɪn/ *adj.* not fat: *You should eat more, you are too* **thin.** p15

think /θɪŋk/ *v.* to use the mind, to have an opinion: *What do you* **think** *of our new teacher?* p36

thirsty /'θɜːstɪ/ *adj.* wanting or needing to drink something. p55

threatening /'θretnɪŋ/ *adj.* makes people feel unpleasant things are possible; opposite **unthreatening**: *His aggressive behaviour was very* **threatening.** p55

thriller /'θrɪlə'/ *n.* a book, play or film that tells an exciting story, usually of crime or violence. p44

tidy /'taɪdɪ/ *adj.* in good order, not untidy: *Your son's room is very* **tidy.** p13

tin /tɪn/ *n.* (or **can**) a container made of metal: *Please buy some* **tins** *of soup from the supermarket.* p96

tip /tɪp/ *v.* to give a small amount of money to someone: *I always* **tip** *the waiter 10%.* **tip** *n.* p25

toaster /'təʊstə'/ *n.* an electric machine for toasting bread. p108

toothbrush /'tuːθbrʌʃ/ *n.* a small brush for cleaning the teeth. p18

toothpaste /'tuːθpeɪst/ *n.* substance used for cleaning the teeth. p64

town /taʊn/ *n.* a large group of houses and other buildings where people live and work. p70

transport /'trænspɔːt/ *n.* a means or system of carrying goods or passengers from one place to another, eg. bus, train, lorry, etc. p20

travel agent /'trævleɪdʒənt/ *n.* a person whose work is to arrange other people's holidays and journeys. p21

traveller's cheque /'trævləztʃek/ *n.* a cheque which can be exchanged abroad for the currency of that country. p18

truth /truːθ/ *n.* (no *pl.*) what is true, the correct facts: *You should always* **tell the truth.** p117

try /traɪ/ *v.* to do one's best to do something: *He* **tried** *to climb the tree but he couldn't.* p36

tube /tjuːb/ *n.* a soft metal or plastic container with a cap: *a* **tube** *of toothpaste.* p96

turn away /tɜːnə'weɪ/ *v.* to look in another direction to show displeasure: *I tried to talk to her, but she* **turned away.** p86

twin /twɪn/ *n.* one of two children born of the same mother at the same time. p13

type /taɪp/ *v.* to use a machine to print letters on paper. p63

typical /'tɪpɪkl/ *adj.* showing the main signs and qualities of a particular group: *Pasta is* **typical** *Italian food.* p57

underground station /'ʌndəgraʊndsteɪʃn/ *n.* a place to catch a train which goes under the ground. p20

understanding /ʌndə'stændɪŋ/ *adj.* sympathetic and kind: *She was very* **understanding** *when I told her my problem.* p25

university /juːnɪ'vɜːsətɪ/ *n.* a place where you can study for a degree after you have left school. p51

use /juːz/ *v.* to do something with; have a purpose for: *What do you* **use** *this machine for?* p63

usually /'juːʒʊəlɪ/ *adv.* done or happening regularly: *I am* **usually** *at work by 8.30 am.* p39

vain /veɪn/ *adj.* too proud of yourself, especially what you look like: *She is very* **vain,** *she is always looking at herself in the mirror.* p55

vegetarian /vedʒə'teərɪən/ *n.* a person who doesn't eat meat. p32

visit /'vɪzɪt/ *v.* to go and see: *We* **visited** *my parents at the weekend.* p27

vote /vəʊt/ *v.* to choose someone secretly during an election. **voter** *n.* the person. p79

walkman /'wɔːkmən/ *n.* a very small machine for playing music which has small earphones and is carried around by the user. p18

war /wɔː'/ *n.* fighting between nations: *The two countries were at* **war** *for many years.* p66

wash up /wɒ'ʃʌp/ *v.* to clean the dishes after a meal. p24

washing machine /'wɒʃɪŋməʃiːn/ *n.* a machine for washing clothes: *Put the clothes in the tumble dryer after taking them out of the* **washing machine.** p108

waste /weɪst/ *v.* to use something wrongly or badly: *Don't* **waste** *time, do your work!* p26

watch /wɒtʃ/
1 *v.* to look at; keep one's eyes on: *Will you* **watch** *the baby while I'm out?* p27
2 *n.* a small clock worn on the wrist. p69

wealth /welθ/ *n.* (no *pl.*) riches; owning a lot of houses, land, etc. **wealthy** *adj.* p67

weapon /'wepən/ *n.* a thing with which we fight, eg. a gun. p106

weather /'weðə'/ *n.* (no *pl.*) the state of the wind, rain, sun, etc.: *I don't like this cold* **weather.** p4

wedding /'wedɪŋ/ *n.* the ceremony when people get married: *I'm going to my brother's* **wedding** *tomorrow.* p120

well /wel/ *adj.* in good health, not ill: *My husband and I are both very* **well,** *thank you.* p9

western /'westən/ *n.* a film about cowboys in the West of the USA. p44

win /wɪn/ *v.* to be first or to do best in a competition, race or fight: *Who* **won** *the football match?* p67

wine /waɪn/ *n.* (no *pl.*) an alcoholic drink made from grapes. p61

worried /'wʌrɪd/ *adj.* anxious: *I'm* **worried** *about my exams.* p68

young /jʌŋ/ *adj.* not having lived very long; not old. p85

zip /zɪp/ *n.* a fastener that is often used on clothes, and has two sets of teeth which can be joined together. p49

Grammar index

Numbers are page numbers. LR means Language Review.